THE GREAT TOURS

VUELTA GIRO TOUR

Graham Watson

THE GREAT TOURS

VUELTA GIRO TOUR

Graham Watson

FOREWORD BY MIGUEL INDURAIN

Without doubt the Vuelta a Espana, Giro d'Italia and Tour de France provide the greatest challenge in a professional cyclist's career. These great national tours represent the culmination of years of hard work, of learning one's weaknesses in order to strengthen, of learning to adapt, and discovering one's most extreme limits as an athlete. And all this just to be able to compete, let alone to even consider winning any one of these great races. The life of a professional racing cyclist is fraught with challenges, of both a physical and emotional nature, and it is in the tours of Spain, Italy and France where these challenges are at their highest, and from where the greatest champions emerge.

Every male cyclist has dreamed of one day riding in the Tour de France, and I suppose I was no different to any other youngster when I rode my first race at the age of eleven in my native Navarra region of Spain, conscious of the fact that Eddy Merckx, the greatest cyclist ever, was at the very height of his powers then, competing in races that seemed so far away from my Villava home at the time. For sure, Merckx was my first cycling hero, perhaps my only one, and I remember reading then about his heroic exploits in the 1975 Tour de France as Merckx battled against a jaw-injury to try for a sixth Tour win. As I began racing seriously a few years later, it was Bernard Hinault who was dominating the sport, and I remember being so impressed by his time-trialling dominance of the Tour de France.

By listening to the older men of our club talking, I learnt of the legends of the other great national tours - the Vuelta and Giro - noting that both Merckx and Hinault had raced well in these races too, while one of my own countrymen, Federico Bahamontes, had put Spanish pride on the map with his Tour victory in 1959. For the past few years it has been me that has dominated the Giro and Tour, though not yet the Vuelta, and now my days as a youthful member of the Villava Cycling Club seem a great distance behind, though I still take an interest in all its activities, knowing how much its membership has swelled along with my successes.

For now, the tours of Spain, Italy and France must remain as the physical challenges they indeed are, in order that I may continue to strive for victory in each of them, yet one day I know that I too will enjoy reading back to the memories of one tour or another, recalling my battles with the men who are now my rivals, but who I know one day, will be my life-long friends. It is for this reason that books like The Great Tours are a wonderful souvenir of this wonderful sport of cycling - and deserve as much acclaim as possible. The author, Graham Watson, is a familiar face on the circuit, and his camera skills are renowned for capturing those special moments in cycling that portray all of us, champions and challengers, as well as the sport as a whole, in such a powerful way.

The life of a cycling photographer is not unlike our own, because photographers are very much a feature of our daily lives as we pedal our way around the countryside, knowing that our movements and emotions are likely to be captured on film for the fans. Sometimes, when I look ahead and see a cluster of motorbike cameramen competing for the best view of our battles, I wonder which occupation is the most hazardous - a cyclist, or a photographer! Yet for the most part they carry out their work with a great deal of respect for us, and for this reason we can respect them too. I hope you enjoy The Great Tours - with sixteen years of experience, the author has some great stories to tell, and some great photography to illustrate it.

Published by Optimus Sport International,
Forge Works, Church Road, Gt Bookham
Surrey, KT23 3JP, England

First edition 1994

British Library Cataloguing in Publication Data
Watson, Graham
Great Tours
I. Title
796.62

ISBN 0-9523445-0-5
Editor: Frances Royle
Design: Beatriz Pi & Blanka Agiriano
Repro: Igara, San Sebastian
Printed and bound in Spain by Printek

Produced by Dorleta, S.A.

INTRODUCTION

This is the one memory that has brought me back to the Vuelta year after year: the Picos de Europa dwarfs the 1985 Vuelta as its leaders approach the finish in los Lagos de Covadonga. (inset): the Monasterio de Covadonga guards our approach..

I can still clearly remember the day: the 29th April 1985. Especially memorable was the place - the Monasterio de Covadonga, set high above the valley of Onís, rising above the forests that cling to the hillsides. The imposing arched roof and twin spires of its church dominated the skyline above Covadonga, as if guarding the approach to the distant mountains just visible beyond. I remember an aura almost of impending doom, so eerily did the church loom through the trees. I'd arrived in Spain for the first time in my life just the day before, and had felt nothing but wonderment at this spectacular country from the moment I stepped foot on

Spanish soil. The landscape, the stunning architecture, the people, especially the buzz of excitement in the streets - it had made such an impression. And now, the climax of my first day on the Vuelta - the road to los Lagos de Covadonga.

The sight of the church should have been an omen of what awaited the climbers - a vicious incline shattering the intact peloton as it emerged from the shadow of the trees. But really nothing could have prepared me for the sight of the Vuelta, out in the open once more, shedding cyclists all over the narrow road that climbed from one promontory to the next, each turn in the road offering a better view of the landscape. All around me raged the phenomenon of the Vuelta - the cars, the motorbikes, the cyclists and the spectators - but surrounding us all the magnificence of the Sierra de Covadonga, a paradise of wild countryside hidden away at the foot of the Picos de Europa. I went to work with increased zeal, spurred on by my glorious

surroundings and by the fervour of the racing - it was a pretty important day for the cyclists too ...

My driver took me on and up; behind, beside and in front of the leading group of cyclists, I filmed their determination to win this the most prestigious stage of the race. I teased the race officials to distraction, tormenting them and their stringent regulations that forbade working in any logical way whatsoever, let alone the way I work - close-up, filming every attack as the leading five riders worked their way up the sinuous climb. Just then, they were the best cyclists in the Vuelta - Delgado, Millar, Rodríguez, Muñoz, and Parra - and they danced up the steep slope as if it were a boulevard, sprinting into each turn like greyhounds and accelerating away like hares. Yet even this masterpiece of athleticism faded before the magnificence waiting around the corner.

Up ahead I saw what seemed to be the summit, and I jumped down from the bike for

the final shot of the day, my attention already distracted by a first glimpse of the spectacular skyline. But instead of stopping there, the race continued, swooping over the crest and down to a plateau of lakes and glowing heather, where - among the thousands of people who awaited the Vuelta - wild ponies roamed free against a backdrop of blue sky and white mountains. By now I was mentally drained, and I took a last, long, lingering look as the Vuelta sped towards the Picos de Europa, the scale of the mountains dwarfing the five cyclists and their motorised entourage as they created dazzling reflections in the glacial lakes. I was content to stand back and let the race go away from me: my body was drenched in the sweat of my exertions; my mind was drowning in the exultant realisation that in Spain I'd discovered the cycling photographer's Aladdin's cave.

Nearly ten years on, and after as many more Vueltas, this is still my most vivid

The *Maglia Rosa* is the sacred image of the Giro d'Italia, and conveniently offers the photographer a pleasant contrast after the *amarillo* of the Vuelta and before the *maillot jaune* of Tour de France. Bruno Leali is the proud race-leader in 1993, leading Stephen Roche on a stage to Asiago in the Dolomites.

A photographers fairly typical view of the mighty Tour de France - Miguel Indurain, just visible through the flanks of the world's media in Montlhery, 1993.

memory of the race. More to the point, it changed my whole outlook on top-level road racing. Until I came to Spain, I'd always assumed that the Tour de France and the classics said all there was to say to the adventurous cycling photographer. But once I'd experienced the Vuelta I decided to see if the Giro d'Italia could be this good too - and I was not to be disappointed. Thereafter, the Tour de France took on another, slightly different, perspective; I was then, and I am still, obliged to photograph the Tour - it is too important to ignore. But I choose to come each year to photograph the Vuelta and the Giro.

There is no more privileged observer of a great tour than a photographer, especially if he is aboard a motor-bike and able to witness - and sometimes share - the very same adventures as the cyclists. These adventures unfold before a backdrop of timeless landscapes that provide the keenest pleasure of following a big race: and the photographer

captures them all on film. Long distance stage-racing embodies the very spirit of cycling with its potent cocktail of gut-wrenching courage and unparalleled athleticism, as well as the sheer exhilaration of travel. And it can be addictive: for both cyclist and *suiveur* a stage-race has all the ingredients of a soap-opera, with its star players - the cyclists - cast as heroes and villains, plodders and high-fliers, according to the requirements of the media-driven plot.

The drama is enacted over several weeks, giving time for each player to assert himself in a leading role - or accept that his role is to watch the show from the wings. In the greatest of them all, the Tour de France, drama competes with exploit and courage, and then again with bare-faced commercialism, to attract a world-wide audience approaching one billion people - and surprisingly, the sporting aspect of the event wins through day after day after long day; the Tour is the father of all cycle

races. But the Vuelta and Giro have, with their rich mixture of sport, heroics and beauty, a subtler attraction for case-hardened race followers. They each last as long as the French race, are often as exciting and - as far as the Vuelta is concerned - far more majestic. They are both far less commercialised, which allows one to enjoy the sporting element within the race. In their different ways each of the three big tours justifies its place in the nine-month long racing season; each race is run at its own pace, moulding its unique character and reputation.

Inevitably, the character of each race tends to reflect the lifestyle of the host nation. If the Vuelta is as wild and passionate as the Spanish people, the Giro is by contrast romantic and dignified. And nothing can quite match the Tour de France for its arrogant nationalism. All three tours take their followers on a thrill-a-minute journey around three of the most romantic countries in Europe, blending culture with courage,

history with agony, beauty with sadness; mixing escapism with sport.

'Escapism' is really the only word to describe life 'on tour'. Most normal people are coping with end-of-winter blues, and summer is still a wistful dream away, when the sap starts to rise in the tour follower. In late April, before the winter snows have melted from the high ground over which must of the race will travel, the Vuelta has its devotees already on the road. When the race ends in mid-May spring has suddenly gone, ousted by the first warmth of summer - though by this time the really serious *aficionado* will already be en route to Italy and the distractions of the Giro. Three weeks of that tour takes you firmly into the summer, and the brief return home before the Tour de France begins merely accentuates the feeling that you really have escaped from normality.

For my part, the attractions of stage-racing are so diverse that it is sometimes difficult to know which one of them gives me most pleasure. Unlike the one-day classics, a stage-race takes time to evolve, opening up new sporting possibilities day after day, fulfilling the wishes of even the most demanding sports enthusiast. Then there is the indescribable pleasure one gets out of moving on day after day, leaving behind the memories of yesterday for the as-yet-unknown adventures of today as fresh scenery, awe-inspiring architecture, and a differing way of life await the working traveller. I have taken great pleasure in wringing every possible gram of enjoyment out of my work, though as a photographer that hasn't been too hard to do!

Apart from the many memories recorded visually in this book there are many more that went unrecorded, either because they happened when a camera wasn't at hand, or were simply unrecordable - as in June 1991, when the entire Giro peloton stopped outside a Sanson factory whose workforce was out in the road dispensing *gelati* to one and all, and Mario Cipollini was seen to have eaten no less than three himself... or again in the Giro, when I uncharacteristically found myself shouting excited encouragement at Miguel Indurain as he continued the attack that SHOULD have won him the 1994 race, so spectacularly did he attack over the Passo del Mortirolo.

Antics in the Vuelta however exceed all others, such as when the unfortunate Vuelta press-officer, José Manuel Egido, was hit by a snowball before a stage-start at Bosost in 1991. That it made contact at all was welcome proof that the previous night's overdose of *Pacharán* hadn't damaged my eyesight, but the fact that somehow the snow got into both of Egido's boots ensures retaliation one day ... or so he keeps threatening. Then there's the fun of travelling for weeks on end with like-minded colleagues, sharing long hours of hard work - yet also taking time to turn bad days into great ones by some serious post-race socializing. This is perhaps the ultimate satisfaction: the camaraderie that grows from shared dramas and crises - as well as the friendships I've made with the cyclists themselves.

The Great Tours is meant to expand upon the celebration of professional cycle racing that was first introduced in *Visions of Cycling*, and later in *The Road to Hell*. In this book I have deliberately placed the emphasis on photography in a far greater way even than *Visions or Hell,* in the hope that the role of photography can be best understood and appreciated - and for the photographs to be enjoyed in their own right. Amongst the majority of the as-yet-unseen pictures in *The*

Great Tours, I have therefore felt obliged to include at least a few of what I consider to be the the real classics of my work; alongside the images of the mid-1990's, the memories of epic tours of the previous decade are too strong to be overlooked. And in providing some technical reference to the photographs, I've stopped short of outright theory so as not to deflect from the prime motivation of my work - for it is the sport that inspires me first, and only then the photography.

The Vuelta is the source of my fondest memories in a tour-career that began a full seven years before I set foot in Spain - in 1977, with my first Tour de France. The Tour's memories are harder to recall, submerged as they probably were by the more serious goings-on in the race. Yet even so there are many, and none more curious

than in 1988, at the height of the controversy over race-leader Pedro Delgado's alleged drug infringements. With the world's press having overplayed the whole affair, Delgado had spent a very uncomfortable few days awaiting a final decision on whether he'd be allowed to finish the Tour. On the day when the Tour's decision was to be made public a posse of photographers was waiting at Delgado's hotel when his team-mates began the ride to the start without him. Though we could see Delgado was dressed and ready to race, the thousands of expectant journalists and fans waiting at the start must have assumed - seeing his team-mates sign on without their leader - that Delgado was quietly withdrawing from the race. The photographers, of course, knew different, and larked around with Delgado as he made his solitary way towards the town centre, enjoying the quiet ride before the expected crush at the start.

Thus it was, with the world's media assembled at the start line looking for him, that Delgado was to be found posing with the motorcycle photographers on the road to Limoges, insisting he have his picture taken with each one of us! It was a bizarre experience;

In between some explosive periods of racing, the Vuelta gives some a chance to relax: Gerhard Zadrobilek was one such person before a stage in 1990, while later that same day, the whole peloton rode like tourists as the ancient ruins of a once mighty castle near Huesca loomed on the skyline.

at the same time, if courage is grace under pressure it proved what a great sportsman Delgado really is. Later, however, when our films were developed, we all had some explaining to do: it wasn't quite the assignment our picture editors had asked for ...

We work in such close proximity to the 'stars' that inevitably photographers can get to know them far better than anyone else. This intimacy lasts down the years, and can stay intact for as long as a cyclist continues to race; occasionally, if a real friendship has developed, longer still. Fifteen years down the road from my first full Tour - won by Bernard Hinault - I've seen the racing careers of men like Hinault, Joop Zoetemelk, Francesco Moser, come to an end, only to find the very same personalities back in the entourage as team managers, PR men or race officials. Closer to home, I've seen the careers of Greg LeMond, Sean Kelly and Stephen Roche in their entirety, and I don't know - so thrilling were their victories in the 1980s - if we'll ever see their like again.

And I've seen the career of Greg LeMond superseded so perfectly by that of Miguel Indurain - whose awesome power first graced my photography in that first Vuelta in 1985 - and Tony Rominger. Indurain is very much a man of the great tours, THE modern tour man in fact, and Rominger is his only challenger - two more perfect cycling athletes there are not. It is men like these who make my work so rewarding, so interesting and satisfying, yet still play just one part in the total enjoyment of photographing stage-racing. Together, the Vuelta, Giro and

Tour contain a world of characters too numerous to mention, of pent-up dramas and emotions, of landscapes too overwhelming to adequately describe, or photograph. It is the combined splendour of these three races that inspires the title of this book, and the photography recorded within. Enjoy it - I know I certainly have.

Limoges, the Tour de France 1988: Delgado poses with the author...

The successes of men like Stephen Roche (right) and Sean Kelly (opposite page), did much for my career in the 1980's.

VUELTA A ESPAÑA

The Vuelta offers a multitude of varying images to the photographer, whether it be the sight of the peloton disintegrating on the green, green hillsides in Cantabria (left), or sights more man-made, like this corny portrait of the diminutive Jesus Montoya in Burgos, 1992. Montoya is the one in shorts...

The first time it had been a simple fuel problem; the second a far more serious oil leak. And now the battered orange motorbike lay on its side in the road again, struck down this time not by mechanical malfunction, but by my inept driver's failure to engage the footrest in time. For the third time in a week, the peloton howled its amusement as it swept past, and I wanted to dig a big hole and hide in it. It shouldn't have happened to me, really it shouldn't, but the chaotic nature of this particular race is legendary: even before I'd joined the Vuelta Ciclista a España for the first time some weeks earlier, I suppose I'd anticipated adventures like this.

To the average holiday-maker, Spain is just a long

21

At just 20 years of age, Miguel Indurain awaits the start of a time trial in Alcala de Henares in 1985.

beach, stretching from the northernmost shores of the Mediterranean to the gates of the Atlantic. Hot sun, white sand, blue skies: it is a paradise for sun-worshippers, and they lie baking their skins by the thousand, oblivious to the delights of the hinterland. To me, Spain seemed the most underrated country in Europe, a nation of colourful people inhabiting an even more colourful landscape of apparently limitless beauty, all on display and accessible in her national tour.

My acquaintance with the Vuelta began in 1985, on a

scorching hot afternoon in the northern city of Oviedo. Or perhaps it really started early that morning, on the rattly old bus from Bilbao to Oviedo - a bus whose driver took an unscheduled *siesta* somewhere along the road, with the result that I missed the finish of that day's stage. It wasn't an auspicious beginning, but I quickly recognised it as typical when the Vuelta, with its characteristic style of pandemonium, got into its stride.

Inevitably, national Tours tend to reflect the character of the people and their way of life. Nowhere is this more so than in the case of the Vuelta, as those first few days in northern Spain clearly illustrated. On the one hand there was untold kindness and goodwill from the people responsible for my hospitality and day-to-day arrangements; on the other, apparent hostility from many race officials, even some of the race directors, who clearly failed to see why any foreign photographer should be remotely interested in the race: '... and we'd rather you weren't here ...' seemed to sum up their attitude. In fact I was only there at all at the behest of a Spanish publisher, who intended to use my pictures of the Vuelta in the inaugural issue of a new Spanish cycling magazine!

The arrangements for my rendezvous with my new client were as fraught with the potential for mishap as everything else on the race. I was to stand as close to the finish line as possible, with a copy of *Winning* magazine in my hand, and I would be met by one of a group of people I'd never set eyes on, who would be carrying a similar form of identification. In any country other than

Spain it might have worked ... Thanks to my bus driver, I arrived just as stage-winner Federico Echave was mounting the podium, which was surrounded by a small matter of tens of thousands of people who had swarmed onto the road after the finish. Two hours later, having been bullied from the finish area by the Guardia Civil and twice misdirected around Oviedo, I finally made contact. From then on my fortunes fluctuated wildly, depending on the degree of the chaos, the nature of my requests, the obduracy of the race officials, and the incompetence on any particular day of one Señor Ortega, the driver of the 500cc Benelli selected to haul my 75-kilo carcass around Spain - quite inadequately, as it turned out.

Ortega apart, in those days there was a lot to be said for following the Vuelta by motorbike, not least the freedom to dispense with a crash helmet - a freedom as exhilarating as the breeze that rushed around my head. But the price of that freedom was the continual risk of injury: barely had next day's stage set off down the road than a motorbike pile-up left me doubtful about reaching the finish that day, let alone Salamanca in a few weeks' time. Never had I seen such a range of driving skills aboard such a dubious array of machinery, and in the days that followed a score of mishaps involving motorbikes punctuated the progress of the race, leaving me amazed that no cyclist had been injured.

It was in the Vuelta that I first sampled sitting on a motorbike facing backwards, seeing part of the country I'd just passed through rather than that which I

was about to, had I been facing the 'correct' way. And viewing the action continuously was a novelty in its own right. Instead of twisting around every few seconds to see what was happening, here I sat and divulged the whole show, enjoying an uninterrupted view of the action in what was for me a slightly self-conscious affair. Nobody can enjoy seeing men suffer, even if this variety was doing so of its own choosing, and in an athletical arena where suffering is the norm rather than the extraordinary. Even so, not being able to turn away when the agony of the cyclists was so evident made for a very uncomfortable time,

and I was glad when, a few years later, this style of working was banned by safety-conscious officials.

In any major race, the motorized entourage can be an added attraction to roadside spectators. In the Vuelta, this attraction degenerates into a 'hell on wheels', with television motorbikes, radio-station motorbikes, photographers' motorbikes and officials' motorbikes coming together in a great explosion of horsepower whose ferocity is matched only by the team-car drivers and the 40-odd bikes from the Guardia Civil. It was little wonder that my Vuelta that year produced so little actual photography,

In 1992, a car from Spanish television crashed just ahead of the descending peloton on the road to Gijon. A cameraman from the same station dutifully films the scene for posterity. The car had been pointing the other way until it hit a brick wall...

working as I was in the teeth of official obstruction and dangerous driving, and with the added distraction of nannying Señor Ortega and his dilapidated machine through their first-ever cycle race ...

Yet out of the ruins of those first few days grew an adventure as exciting as anything I've yet to experience. Everything about the Vuelta is as crazy, as romantic, and as vibrant as Spain herself, and I was simply swept along in its wake, powerless to resist the explosive energy of the race and its *aficionados*. The Vuelta is passionate and romantic far beyond anything the Giro or Tour has to offer, and its relative obscurity only strengthens its attraction to those of us in the know. One can only hope Spain's recent emergence as a major cycling nation doesn't do for the romance of the Vuelta what package tours did for the Mediterranean coast.

Working on the Vuelta in the fickle spring climate is one of the great challenges of the season. From one day to the next the weather can change dramatically: from a 40-degree heatwave across the plain of Castilla y León, to a sub-zero snowstorm in the Pyrenees, testing my camera, and my constitution, to the limit. In 1991 I found myself standing in a freezing cloud a few thousand feet up at Valdezcaray where, though I could barely see them, twelve-foot-high

banks of snow completely dwarfed the time triallists as they scrabbled their uncertain way up the narrow muddy track in atrocious conditions. And this straight after a warm, sun-drenched Amstel Gold race in the Netherlands: it could only happen in the Vuelta ...

The Vuelta, following hard on the heels of a series of one-day classics in northern Europe, can be an uncomfortable proposition in a number of respects. Twice-weekly stints on the motorbike are replaced by a more demanding daily workload that lasts for weeks on end, with no respite until the finish is reached. And the slick, no-nonsense organisation of the classics is unknown in Spain. Fortunately, the pictures I get in a typical Vuelta often turn out to be the most dramatic and beautiful of the season, with acute contrasts of terrain

and weather only surpassed by the contrasts between fit and not-so-fit cyclists as they come to terms with a three-week-long stage race.

For the cyclists too, the Vuelta is a spectacular turning point in the season, coming early in the year when a series of one-day races has failed to put adequate mileage into their legs. Many top cyclists use the Vuelta as preparation for one of the summer tours - the Giro or Tour - but for others it is the single most important event of the season. This is of course especially so for the Spaniards; but often only the Colombians - at least in their hey-days of the 1980's - have been 'Vuelta-fit' thanks to racing and training at altitude in Colombia.

The Vuelta is unique in that so many more Colombians take part than in the other great tours; in fact, the Vuelta is as important to the Colombians as the Tour de France is to a Frenchman, and the battle between the diminutive South Americans and their European rivals has often been the highlight of the race, especially if a Fabio Parra or Lucho Herrera was on form in any particular year.

When Herrera flew back to Bogotá a few days after having won the 1987 Vuelta, an estimated half million people turned out to greet him, Colombia's radio stations having broadcast live transmissions from the race during the pre-

Valdezcaray, 1991: Fabio Parra defied the abysmal conditions to win this time trial stage, seemingly oblivious to the mass of snow at his side.

vious three weeks. News of the Vuelta is as much sought after by the Colombians as coverage of an England test series by Australians - and they get it the same way, by staying up all night!

Only two riders - Jacques Anquetil in 1963 and Bernard Hinault in 1978 - have won the Vuelta and the Tour de France in the same year. And only two men - Giovanni Battaglin of Italy and Eddy Merckx of Belgium - have recorded back-to-back doubles of Vuelta and Giro, in 1973 and 1981 respectively, and only then in the knowledge that they were not to attempt the Tour de France as well. These facts alone offer more than a hint of the severity

of the Vuelta, adding another facet to the fascination of the race: is that rider trying to win, or simply preparing for a tour elsewhere?

In 1991, following the failure of his team-mate Pedro Delgado in the previous year's race. Miguel Indurain was goaded by the Spanish press into believing he could win the Vuelta. In the event, he made a mess of it all, suffering irreversible setbacks in the mountains, while his rival and eventual victor, Melchor Mauri, outsped him in every time trial section of the race. Written off by the fickle Spanish press for his inconsistency, Indurain responded by winning the Tour de France in convincing style - benefiting, ironically, from his rigorous preparation in the Vuelta. Thereafter, loth to chance his reputation for invincibility, Indurain has made a point of avoiding the race.

The sporting attraction of the Vuelta lies in determining which of the pre-race favourites is really in with a chance, and the suspense is often drawn out to within a day or two of the finish: the ring of mountains west of

'Lucho' Herrera (below) and Martin Farfan (bottom) are the two other Colombians who, with Parra, enlivened the Vuelta in the late 1980's and early 1990's. Farfan is seen in 1989, on his way to losing his race-lead on the road to Santona.

The noble face of Melchor Mauri looked down on everyone during the 1991 race, not least Miguel Indurain. The Catalunya man wore the *amarillo* jersey for nineteen of the twenty-one stages.

Madrid usually has a decisive influence on the outcome. By then many contenders will have seen their chances dynamited by a 'bad day' in one of Spain's numerous mountain ranges, or by making the wrong effort at the wrong time, in response to a sadistic attack by one of the Colombians. Since courageous riders like Parra, Herrera and Martin Farfán rejuvenated the race with their spirited climbing, Spain's recognised 'big boys' have had to work harder- and often in unaccustomed collaboration - to combat their enemy.

Even though Herrera, Parra and Farfan have now retired, and Colombia at best can only send a half-amateur, half-pro team to the Vuelta, their presence is felt constantly. Colombia's hopes in Spain these days rest with Oliverio Rincon, who graduated from the Colombian-backed, Spanish-based Kelme team into Amaya, and now ONCE. Though Rincón stands alone as Colombia's great hope in Spain, his participation in the Vuelta is still enough to attract

two Colombian radio-stations, the commentators no doubt hoping their investment will one day pay off and that once again a top Colombian team will enter the race. It's not surprising Unipublic - organisers of the Vuelta since 1979 - are trying to tempt the American Motorola team into the 1995 Vuelta, for that will bring Colombia's outright star, Alvaro Mejía, into the arena, thus guarenteeing an increased Colombian presence of media people. The Vuelta without Colombians would be like English county cricket without its band of West Indian batsmen...

Just as Spanish riders have had to adjust to foreign competition, so international media attention means that race officials have at last come to terms with the need for better organisation. The contrast between the 1985 Vuelta - run on somewhat shaky lines to say the least - and the Vuelta of 1994 could not be more marked. The Vuelta of the 1990's is probably better organised than the Tour de France, and yet - thankfully - still manages to

retain its spontaneous character. There are also big competitive differences between the editions of 1985 and 1994 - the Vuelta is at its incomparable best when a home-grown talent is at least in contention, and for all the admirable qualities of Tony Rominger or Alex Zülle, their struggle for domination does not compare with the battles between Robert Millar and Pedro Delgado in '85, or between Delgado and Parra in 1989.

It was only in the early 1980s that foreign teams started racing the Vuelta en masse, attracted largely by the prize money on offer from an administration keen to bring Spain back into the modern, commercial world. Pre-1970s, riders like Jacques Anquetil, Raymond Poulidor, Felice Gimondi and Roger Pingeon had included the Vuelta to their list of victories, though usually against poor opposition, and often vowing never to ride it again, so poorly was the race organised. But like Eddy Merckx, who rode and won his only Vuelta in 1973, each champion of his generation has felt the need to include the Vuelta in his winning portfolio at least once, despite the perils once attached to competing in the race.

Influenced by the example of Belgium's Freddy Maertens, who blitzed the 1977 Vuelta with thirteen stage wins, Spanish sponsors awoke to the attraction of teams that combined Spain's emerging cycling talent with the best men in the world, a formula that provoked interest and speculation amongst the partisan public and increased support for the riders and teams. Maertens' achievements - he also won the race overall - prompted a mini-invasion of foreigners into the Vuelta and, eventually, into Spanish teams; by the mid-eighties, nearly every Spanish team included at least one foreigner. This trend simply mirrored what was happening in every sphere of Spanish life at that time: after years of isolation, Spain was opening her doors to the big wide world. With this growth came unprecedented support from television, which in turn has set up the Vuelta as the country's biggest annual sporting event, a factor that helped attract a record 126 foreigners into the race in 1990.

Foreign sprinters always influence the big gallops in the Vuelta, though not as spectacularly as Mario Cipollini in 1994. In a battle at Salamanca with team-mate Adriano Baffi, Cipollini crashed badly on his first stage of the race, incredibly survirving without serious injury.

27

And the Spanish teams' investment has paid off: since 1977 there has been a string of victories by foreign riders in Spanish teams: Sean Kelly in 1988 - in a KAS jersey; Marco Giovanetti in 1990 - in a SEUR jersey; and latterly Rominger, riding for CLAS. The successor to Rominger may well be another foreigner, Alex Zülle, the bespectacled Swiss from the ONCE team which includes by far the most foreigners. Watching the militaristic deployment of the ONCE team in the Vuelta

is one of my spring treats. Having enjoyed their traditional domination of the early-season races, and felt the air of expectancy that envelops the team as it heads home for the Vuelta in April, I find their calculated approach comical in a race so unpredictable, and maybe it is no coincidence that it is CLAS and Banesto who often win through - a reflection that perhaps in Spain, it is better to live and race like the natives.

The life-story of the Vuelta is as diverse as that of the

country. In the two editions that were held before the start of the Civil War in 1937, the field was as comparatively international as it is now, with French, Dutch, Swiss, Italian, Austrian and Belgian riders all taking on the home stars in a field of just 50 riders. It was a Belgian, Gustav Deloor, who carried off the *amarillo* jersey with convincing wins on both occasions. Under the Franco regime the race resumed in 1941 - ironically, the rest of the world was now at war - and the field was entirely Spanish save for four Swiss cyclists, presumably claiming the same neutrality as their 28 opponents in order to fight a war *a la bicicleta.*

Only in 1955, after the Vuelta had endured three different organisers, did it host a truly international field again, this time under the patronage of the fascist-funded newspaper, El Correo Español del Pueblo Vasco. Starting and finishing in Bilbao, sixty Spaniards lined up against forty-seven foreigners - six of whom made up the British team - and it was one of the two French teams that provided the winner in Jean Dotto. The next three years saw the emergence of Federico Bahamontes as a major force in

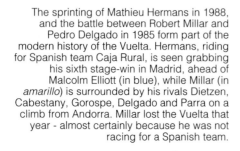

The sprinting of Mathieu Hermans in 1988, and the battle between Robert Millar and Pedro Delgado in 1985 form part of the modern history of the Vuelta. Hermans, riding for Spanish team Caja Rural, is seen grabbing his sixth stage-win in Madrid, ahead of Malcolm Elliott (in blue), while Millar (in *amarillo*) is surrounded by his rivals Dietzen, Cabestany, Gorospe, Delgado and Parra on a climb from Andorra. Millar lost the Vuelta that year - almost certainly because he was not racing for a Spanish team.

cycling, though for his national tour the 'eagle of Toledo' never managed to find the form that would win him the Tour de France in 1959.

At that time, the Basque region dominated the Vuelta, with either Bilbao, or its more cosmopolitan neighbour San Sebastian, hosting the start or finish of the race fourteen times in seventeen years. And Basque riders, although they never managed to come up with an overall winner, dominated the peloton. But Franco's death in 1975 opened the floodgates on an outpouring of suppressed Basque nationalism, and in 1978 fanatical Basque separatists bombed the roads of the penultimate

stage of the Vuelta, scaring the organisers into cancelling the final time-trial stage next day - and making sure that the Basque region has never hosted the race since.

Basque enthusiasm for cycling refuses to be stifled, however, and their distinctive green, red and white flag can be seen waving dementedly at races all over Europe. At home, they travel in their thousands to cheer on their heroes. In 1990 I stood at the side of the road to Valdezcaray, deafened by tens of thousands of Basque enthusiasts lining the 14-kilometre ascent - the Valdezcaray time trial being the closest the Vuelta got to the Basque country that year. They were

The victory of Marco Giovannetti in 1990 was the 25th success by a foreigner in forty-five Vueltas, a series now heavily extended by Tony Rominger's three consecutive wins.

there to support each and every Basque cyclist on his way to the wind-blown summit, but the main target of their vociferous support was Marino Lejarreta, the most popular Basque cyclist of all time, now on his way to the top.

As I watched him approach the hairpin bend where I stood, it occurred to me that the man from Berriz would have done a darn sight better than his 22nd place that day if he hadn't had to fend off so many pushes! His arrival at the bend went unrecorded on film: I just stood there gaping, camera forgotten, as through the torrential rain appeared Lejarreta plus a stocky figure running alongside him holding an umbrella. Clearly a man entitled to the original derivation of the word 'fan', he managed to protect his *icon* from the elements for over three hundred metres on a 15% gradient ... It was a sight worth watching, not filming, I told myself later, conscious that I'd missed a really extraordinary picture.

Allowing for the extraordinary is a basic survival technique for working on the Vuelta. At every turn in the road, I have the feeling that something is just about to happen that could transform my day completely, and not necessarily for the better! Losing the use of that old battered Benelli for more hours a day than I care to remember was one such example, as was an incident in the 1993 Vuelta. We were ahead of the race and there was an impromptu roadside *fiesta* in the Rioja village of Galilea. My driver Ismael had proudly parked his smart blue BMW close to the festivities, looking on enviously as the press corps gulped down the local wines from a *porrón*. The race passed by en route to Logroño, and we returned to the bike to find that the ignition key was missing ... It was only thanks to a helpful local mechanic, a pair of wire-cutters, and considerable ingenuity, that we were able to by-pass the electronic ignition and re-join the race, forty minutes late.

Other catastrophes are the result of my own lack of foresight. In 1993, at a point in the race when it was clear that Tony Rominger of CLAS was going to win, I arranged to photograph Rominger and all seven of his bikes at Covadonga. My mistake was to select the great *plaza* in front of the church for the shot: viewing the empty square at 8.30 in the morning I had not considered

The ONCE team managed to get it right in the 1991 Vuelta, completely dominating the racing without once relinquishing the race-lead. Manager, Manolo Saiz (left) helps celebrate the team's victory in Madrid, a few hours after his cyclists did the same on the road from Collado Villalba.

The media are everywhere in the Vuelta: while a doctor tends to an injured cyclist, a TVE cameraman moves in to film the agony.

the possibility that it might fill up later. Rominger was due to arrive at 9.30; well before time we had all the bikes in position, obligingly held by a CLAS mechanic. Then five busloads of tourists drew up outside the famous church and started milling around my carefully composed photo shoot, delighted at this unexpected side-show to their visit! Minutes later Rominger arrived, dressed in his *amarillo* jersey, ready for the start of the next stage. I began to sweat; knowing how Rominger hates crowds, and had been mobbed every day on the race, I had visions of him refusing to even get out of his car and my credit with the CLAS team hitting an all-time low. To my enormous relief, he not only got out of the car but co-operated calmly while I attempted to salvage some of the pictures I'd planned - all the time battling with a hundred or more unexpected extras ...

The day of our near-fiasco at Galilea had ended with an example of the way that the partisan Spanish press can allow the race to go to their heads. On the climb to los Lagos de Covadonga, with Rominger's small group in the lead, a certain Spanish photographer had been seen towing a certain Spanish cyclist up the climb, using his motorbike to pace the rider clear of Rominger. After the stage, the international jury issued the photographer with the most severe warning possible, short of expulsion from the race. Less fortunate was a radio motorbike driver, who was expelled for trying to 'interfere' with the outcome of the race. That these were not isolated examples is demonstrated by that day's list of wayward cameramen, which comprised twelve names - though fortunately not mine. Now that was a contrast with 1985!

There is very rarely a Vuelta that doesn't have one particular incident of note that sets it apart from all other memories in a season, and one that always, always, reminds one of exactly which country one's in ... Such was the case in 1989, as Pedro Delgado approached the end of the race with an unassailable lead, and Spanish adulation of their sporting hero reached fever-pitch. For years, Delgado and his Navarra-based team had been the butt of a cantankerous cycling commentator, José Maria García. This vendetta reached its peak with Delgado's drug-drama of the 1988 Tour de France - Garcia, of course, insisting vehemently that Delgado had cheated - and relations between Delgado and Garcia remained cool, to say the least. So Garcia experienced pangs of unpleasant anticipation as the 1989 Vuelta approached Segovia, birthplace and residence of one Pedro Robledo Delgado, the *numero uno* sporting hero of Spain.

For days, rumours had been rife that Garcia and his team of technicians would discreetly leave the race for a few days, at least until Segovia was a few hundred kilometres behind. Yet they stayed on doggedly, in the face of increasing abuse and hostility from spectators along the way, and specifically against the wishes of the Guardia Civil who were responsible for everyone's safety. Only with Segovia practically in sight did Garcia finally relent, though only to the extent of swapping his distinctive red and white cars and motorbikes for unmarked vehicles. And wherever Garcia went, there did a pair of burly security guards go too, sharing with him some very genuine animosity from Delgado's fans. For days before the race reached Segovia, overnight in the town, and especially when it left for Madrid, the route was emblazoned with anti-Garcia propaganda, the worst form of which showed him as a tiny character

Segovia is the place to be when the Vuelta hits town, unless you are not a Pedro Delgado fan...

Pedro Delgado took the time to call home during the 1990 race, using a photographer's mobile phone, for the two obviously have a special relationship... Note this photographer's now illegal stance - facing backwards, and without a helmet!.

being hanged in a crude form of graffiti draped from the city's famous Roman aqueduct.

Such bad feeling is the result of the passionately partisan nature of Spanish cycling fans, and is rare in the Vuelta; on the contrary it is the most sporting of all the three major tours. And the great thing about the Vuelta these days, as opposed to the Tour, or even the Giro, is that the organisers really want you there, want to help you do your work - a far cry from 1985. And

even when there are problems, such as on crowded climbs like los Lagos de Covadonga, or the equally congested ascent to Alto del Naranco, disputes are forgotten almost before the stage has ended. There is a lot of good sport to be had photographing the Vuelta, be it on the narrow climbs to a finish that are characteristic of the race, or the wide-open plains where the sun can burn you to a cinder, and where the wind - or the ONCE team - can rip a peloton to shreds. Compared to the regimented nature of the Tour de France, the Vuelta exudes a freedom that inspires good photography; if ever the Vuelta were to develop the claustrophobia of the Tour de France, a lot of its natural charisma would be lost for good.

Public adulation for the race is spontaneous, usually respectful, at its worst, overwhel-

ming; always astonishing. As the race passes through any decent-sized city or town, it's hard not to take your eyes away from the race and up to the balconies, packed with people cheering madly at the speeding mass, or throwing streamers over the Vuelta and its followers. And to find yourself sharing a hotel with one of the favourite Spanish teams is a flattering nightmare, with hundreds of screaming kids packing the lobby, and thousands more crowded outside, hoping for a glimpse, or autograph, or both, of any passing 'star'.

All along the roadsides, thousands upon thousands of people line up to watch the race go by. Many have been waiting for hours, sitting quietly in a wicker chair watching the world go by, or perched precariously on a giant farm vehicle, whose operator will do little in the way of work today ... Many more

simply find themselves caught up in the road closures that ensure the race's safe progress, yet all of them gladly relinquish what little hurry they were in and wait patiently to see the Vuelta go by. What they see is one of the most extraordinary bike races in the world, in one of the most extraordinary countries in the world. There is nothing else quite like it ...

The ascent to Alto del Naranco is always an explosive affair, with seemingly half the population of the city of Oviedo packed on to its six-kilometre climb. It's not too steep either - which is how this loyal Delgado fan, complete with out-of-date Reynolds jersey, has managed to run alongside his hero in 1992.

This swashbuckling character is Alvaro Pino, winner of the 1986 Vuelta - and victory over the man just to his right, Scotland's Robert Millar. When I first saw Pino, he reminded me of one of those pirates in an old Hollywood movie, with a complexion so dark, his eyes seemed to contain nothing but mystery and danger - a façade intensified even more by the contrast of his skin with the amarillo jersey. Taken under a baking hot sun in southern Spain, fill-in flash has accentuated the feeling of intense heat and effort. In fact, both men are sauntering along in the middle of the peloton, happy to let me and my driver, Rafa Landa, into their private world for a few moments.

CAMERA
Mamiya 1000 RS
LENS
70 mm Mamiya
FILM
100 ASA
SHUTTER
1/500 flash
APERTURE
f 5.6

I caught this unusual portrait of Martin Farfan and Fabio Parra at the height of their escape to Estación de Cerler in 1988. It is very rare to find oneself alongside any cyclist just as he reaches for his bottle - but two cyclists at the same time..?. The moment was lost in a few short seconds, and though many other shots of the two were taken in the minutes that led to Farfan's eventual stage-win - this is the one that counts!.

CAMERA
Bronica ETRs
LENS
75 mm Zenza
FILM
100 ASA
SHUTTER
1/500 flash
APERTURE
f 5.6

I can't resist shots like this... The 1992 Vuelta is climbing the lower slopes of the Col du Peyresourde, during a two-stage diversion into France, and as nothing much is happening strategically, my eyes are on something to identify the Spanish race with French scenery. It's not just chance that I've arrived at this spot a few minutes ahead of the peloton - for I knew this stretch of the valley from a recent Tour de France. Had this been the Tour, I would never have had the freedom of mind neccesary to quit the close-environment of the race and seek a location such as this - and there's no snow up there in July anyway!.

CAMERA
Bronica ETRs
LENS
75 mm
FILM
50 ASA
SHUTTER
1/250
APERTURE
f 5.6

Castles are eveywhere in Spain, and frequently appear on the horizon as the Vuelta passes through the country. The most splendidly preserved example has to be in Avila, a regular stopover point for the race, which provided me with this memorable backdrop in 1994. In order to capture this scene, it meant missing the finish that day, following the main group instead so as to gain maximum impact as the thousands of spectators cheered the Vuelta into the walled city. Just look at the size of the crowd stacked up against the fortress!.

CAMERA
Bronica ETRs
LENS
75 mm Zenza
FILM
50 ASA
SHUTTER
1/500
APERTURE
f 5.6

41

Alex Zulle tried so hard to win the 1993 Vuelta, his chances undoubtedly ruined by a descending crash in the last week. The Swiss cyclist wore the *amarillo* jersey for the first two weeks but lost it on the stage to La Sierra de la Demanda. Zulle is seen on the climb there, responding to an attack by Tony Rominger in the final five-kilometres. The rider clinging to Zulle's pace is Spain's Laudelino Cubino.

CAMERA
Bronica ETRs
LENS
75 mm Zenza
FILM
50 ASA
SHUTTER
1/500 flash
APERTURE
f 5.6

Tony Rominger sets the pace at Los Lagos de Covadonga in 1993, leading Alex Zulle, Laudelino Cubino and Jesus Montoya in pursuit of Pedro Delgado who attacked a few moments earlier. Under a heavily overcast sky, I've opted for using available light rather than fill-in flash which would have lost the natural atmosphere this photograph portrays. And the use of fairly long telephoto lens has allowed me to home in on Rominger's haunted expression as the weather, the climb, and his efforts to win this prestigious stage, begin to show.

CAMERA
Nikon F4
LENS
180 mm
FILM
400 ASA
SHUTTER
1/250
APERTURE
f 2.8

45

Two days after Los Lagos, Tony Rominger launched his big
attack of the 1993 Vuelta, accelerating on the atrocious
descent of the Alto de la Corbetoria, an act that led to Zulle
crashing as his nerve went on the rain-soaked roads.
Rominger is seen on the final ascent to Alto del Naranco, his
face bloated by the effort, and by the rain, as spectators
cheer his impressive escape. Behind him the effort was
being felt by Erik Breukink, who is seen racing flat-out in
pursuit, desperately trying to bridge the near two-minutes
gap for the green jersied Zulle. These two pictures are both
taken with fill-in-flash, which has illuminated the cyclists'
weather-beaten faces, and balanced the reflection thrown up
from the wet roads.

CAMERA
Bronica ETRs
LENS
75 mm Zenza
FILM
50 ASA
SHUTTER
1/500 flash
APERTURE
f 4

CAMERA
Nikon FKE
LENS
85 mm
FILM
200 ASA
SHUTTER
1/250 flash
APERTURE
f 3.5

CAMERA
Bronica ETRs
LENS
75 mm
FILM
100 ASA
SHUTTER
1/250 flash
APERTURE
f 4

Tony Rominger was in *amarillo* again in 1994, wearing the leader's jersey for the entire race. His only challenger was Mikel Zarrabeitia of Spain, whose big effort to challenge Rominger came at Los Lagos at the start of the last week. It was strange to encounter the famous ascent in thick fog, and actually seeing the battle was hard enough - let alone trying to focus on the action. But the eerie conditions showed another side to the mountain's character, as this photograph clearly illustrates.

Marino Lejarreta has twice been a stage winner at Los Lagos de Covadonga and his arrival on the mountain is always greeted enthusiastically by his adoring Basque fans. Here in 1991, Lejarreta is seen at the start of the real climb, tracked by race-leader Melchor Mauri (in *amarillo*), Pello Ruiz-Cabestany, with a young Oliverio Rincon following in 'the master's' wheeltracks. By lying in a ditch, I've managed to get a lower angled shot than would normally be possible, and this definitely adds impact to the riders' expressions.

CAMERA
Bronica ETRs
LENS
75 mm
FILM
50 ASA
SHUTTER
1/500 flash
APERTURE
f 5.6

Djadmoline Abdujaparov
is a regular competitor in
the Vuelta,and has won
many stages in the race,
always with his famous
sprint. He was seen at
his best in 1993 when he
won three of the flat
stages, including this
one at Zaragoza. The
Vuelta is a fairly 'safe'
hunting ground for
Abdu'. for the wide
boulevards used for
most of the finishes
mean he has room to
manouvre his
extraordinary body
without causing injury to
himself- or anybody else
for that matter.

CAMERA
Nikon F4
LENS
300 mm
FILM
200 ASA
SHUTTER
1/500
APERTURE
f 4

This was a lasting image of the 1991 Vuelta. Jean-Paul Van Poppel is winning the third of his four stage-wins that year, but it's the emotions of the cyclist behind him that tell the real story. As lead-out man for Van Poppel, John Talen has seen to it that the PDM team have taken the first three places that day, thanks to an unprecedented exhibition of speed, guile and co-ordination as the race arrived in Zaragoza. Little wonder the loyal domestique feels the need to share Van Poppel's victory...

CAMERA
Nikon F4
LENS
300 mm Nikkor
FILM
100 ASA
SHUTTER
1/500
APERTURE
f 4

CAMERA
Bronica ETRs
LENS
75 mm Zenza
FILM
50 ASA
SHUTTER
1/500 flash
APERTURE
f 5.6 / f 8

Descending is one of the least illustrated facets of cycle-racing as it is extremely difficult to get near the cyclists as they scream down mountainsides at break-neck speed. The Vuelta affords the occassional chance for photographers, thanks to the quality and width of some of Spain's roads. Eduardo Chozas was one of the craziest descenders in the business, and his skills downhill were to help him win a couple of Tour de France mountain stages during his career - gaining most of his advantage on the descents, rather than the climbs!. He is seen here (left) in descending mode during the 1992 Vuelta, crouching ever lower to stave off the challenge of another mad descender, Thomas Wegmüller. Others, such as Britain's Malcolm Elliott (above) sometimes need to risk all to get back to the peloton. Having been dropped on a vicious ascent near Pamplona in 1992, the glamourous sprinter flew down the other side and was quickly back with his mates. "'Hey Malcolm", I yelled', "you're doing 112-kilometres-an-hour!"'. "Oh yeah?"', he replied later, "just make sure you tell people I was attacking at the time, OK?.."

CAMERA
Bronica ETRs
LENS
75 mm Zenza
FILM
50 ASA
SHUTTER
1/500 flash
APERTURE
f 5.6 / f 8

Driving alongside cyclists on a descent is one thing - driving just ahead is another thing altogether. We are on the swoop down from Alto de los Leones in 1992, on the last stage of the Vuelta into Madrid. Everyone's happy, not least Pedro Delgado, who led this last-day exhibition of speed and madness... Thanks to my driver, Ismael Borges, we are just a few yards in front of Perico, and the Spaniard trusted Ismael enough to play in our slipstream - at about 115-kilometres-an-hour! - all the way down the mountain. Seeing the fun he was having, others joined in too, and we soon had faster descenders for company, notably Señor Chozas, the fastest of them all...

CAMERA
Nikon F4
LENS
135 mm Nikkor
FILM
100 ASA
SHUTTER
1/500
APERTURE
f 8

Pedro Delgado had to fight hard to win the 1989 Vuelta, most especially against the Colombian, Fabio Parra. Delgado's emotions show the effort he made at Branillin (above), as he succeeded in putting a few valuable seconds into his rival on the steep run-in. The flambouyant 'Master of Ceremonies', Felipe de Sainz de Trápaga waits to grab the Spanish hero who has clearly given his all.

Melchor Mauri was in another league during the 1991 Vuelta, winning both individual time trials, and leading his team to victory in two team tests against the clock. Mauri is one of the most stylish cyclists around as well, and this portrait of him at Valladolid seems to sum up his overall presentation - as a perfectionist. I tend to go for a lot of cornering shots in time trials as it is the best way to show all the modern components and clothing used in the sport these days. It is also the most flattering way to portray a cyclist - his mental and physical composure is at its most exciting when arched over on a curve in the road.

CAMERA
Nikon F3
LENS
85 mm
FILM
200 ASA
SHUTTER
1/250
APERTURE
f 4

CAMERA
Bronica ETRs
LENS
75 mm Zenza
FILM
50 ASA
SHUTTER
1/500 flash
APERTURE
f 5.6

From Glory to Defeat - Robert Millar's 1985 Vuelta

Robert Millar was clearly the strongest cyclist in the 1985 Vuelta, attacking on all the major climbs, like Los Lagos de Covadonga, to put himself into the race-lead after eleven days.

By the time trial at Alcalá de Henares, Millar had done enough to win, and showed his exuberance for the first time, having established a ten-seconds advantage over Colombia's Pacho Rodriguez, and one-minute and fifteen seconds over Pello-Ruiz Cabestany, winner of the 42-kilometres time trial.

Then it all went wrong for Millar, as Pedro Delgado slipped away on the next day's penultimate stage to Segovia, teaming up with fellow-escapee Jose Recio to build a huge lead - enough to take Delgado from 6th-place overall, more than six minutes behind, into the race-lead - unless Millar reacted.

But Millar knew little of the fact that Delgado had escaped, kept virtually uninformed by his team-mates or manager until it was too late. By the time he did realise the danger of what was happening, he had only his nearest rivals for company - and neither Rodriguez, leading, nor Cabestany, following, had any intention of helping Millar save the race; for they both rode for Spanish teams.

It fell to Millar to chase, and he is seen here on the Alto de los Leones still marked by Rodriguez, and by Fabio Parra, who was clearly part of this combine against the Scot. Now revealing his amarillo jersey after a cold, cold day, Millar's face shows his reluctant acceptance of what's happened to him.

In Segovia, Delgado and Cabestany congratulate themselves on a job well done, with Delgado now the race-leader, and effective winner, over a shocked Millar. Millar's outlook on the sport changed from that very day, and probably stopped him achieving his full potential in the years to come.

61

Pello-Ruiz Cabestany was one of the few people able to speak English to me in my first few Vueltas. The Basque cyclist grabbed my camera during a stage from Albacete in 1986 and, using Pedro Delgado as an improvised model, showed he had skills beyond that of a top cyclist; when I had the films processed, I was suprised that all his shots were sharp, well exposed...and, well, let's hope he sticks to riding a bicycle for as long as I am a photographer... The two clowns on the right are both Italian - well, what would you expect?. To celebrate the end of the 1991 Vuelta, Stefano Giuliani abandoned his bike as the last stage rolled out of Segovia, and jumped up onto the back of Mario Scirea. The pair proceeded to overtake the hysterical peloton, and actually rode along for a few kilometres, until race-officials - and probably Scirea too - had had enough

CAMERA
Nikon F3
LENS
105 mm Nikkor
FILM
100 ASA
SHUTTER
1/250
APERTURE
f 4

CAMERA
Bronica ETRs
LENS
75 mm Zenza
FILM
50 ASA
SHUTTER
1/500 flash
APERTURE
f 5.6 / f 8

There is nothing like the last day in the Vuelta to bring out the best in a professional cyclist... Following a long tradition of such antics, Erwin Nijboer and Alfonso Gutierrez swopped bikes on the stage to Ferrol in 1993. The tallest, and one of the smallest cyclists in the peloton, had everyone laughing as Gutierrez tried in vain to get his right leg over Nijboer's saddle...while the Dutchman himself looks in danger of damaging at least one of his precious knees. Getting shots like this are a heaven-sent oppurtunnity for the seasoned photographer, who wants something more from a race than just men racing each other on bicycles. Often these photographs only comes as a result of having a good rapport with the entertainers concerned.

CAMERA
Bronica ETRs
LENS
75 mm Zenza
FILM
100 ASA
SHUTTER
1/250 flash
APERTURE
f 4

GIRO D'ITALIA

Robert Millar and Eddy Schepers ride shotgun for race-leader Stephen Roche, on the climb up to the Passo Marmolada in 1987.

The scene unfolding before my eyes took a while to assimilate, so unreal did it seem. Fifteen cyclists on the fourteen kilometre ascent of the Marmolada, and twists of pink newspaper flying through the air; an expression of hatred as vivid as the faces of those who were hurling both the newspapers and the abuse. And finally, disgustingly, a distinct spurt of white saliva aimed at the object of hatred. This wasn't a race-riot, nor a workers' revolt: it was the sixteenth stage of the 1987 Giro d'Italia, and we were witnessing one of the most astonishing scenes in modern cycling as the riders ran the gauntlet through an immense crowd, sometimes ten deep, up the Passo Marmolada in the Dolomites. Fourteen cyclists ran the gauntlet; immunity was granted to Italy's Roberto Visentini.

Until the day before, Visentini had been race-leader, lauded and idolised all over Italy since he beat an injured Stephen Roche in the 46-kilometre time trial at San Marino and took from him the hallowed *maglia rosa*. Roche was one of the fourteen subjected to the abuse of Visentini's *tifosi*, indeed the main object of their venom. For the previous day Roche had done the unthinkable, by attacking his own team leader and beating Visentini into the finish at Sappada to 'steal' back his precious race-lead.

The post-race furore had been unprecedented, with spectators, press - even some carabinieri - jostling Roche to demand why he had acted so. Roche, with the bravado that only Irishmen seem able to muster at such times, inflamed Italian tempers by saying he didn't feel Visentini had a God-given right to his support; that Visentini hadn't been good enough to lead the Giro d'Italia anyway; and he felt sure the Italian public were on his side. His explanation failed to calm the growing hostility that included most of his own team-mates and even the Carrera manager, Davide Boifava, who was quoted as saying Roche might be thrown off the team before the next day's start.

That night Roche locked himself into his hotel room with his one loyal team-mate, Eddy Schepers, while outside a

The Passo di Gardena, 1993.

Roberto Visentini arrives in Sappada. Just in time to see Roche receive the new race-leader's jersey on the podium above. He doesn't look too happy, does he..? The next day it was Canazei (below), and Millar shares the podium with Roche who's having fun teasing the *tifosi* in their moments of gloom.

crowd of locals, speculative journalists and the odd policeman looked for all the world like a lynch-mob. In the morning, the cause of all the fuss was to be found calmly chatting with journalists at the start as if nothing untoward had occurred. Visentini, meanwhile, continued to muster Italian sympathy by telling anyone who cared to listen how badly he'd been treated. That Roche was still in the race was down to a midnight visit by the sponsor himself, who insisted that Roche be allowed to lead the team next day. And thus it was that next day we found ourselves trailing Roche's group on the Marmolada, about 75-kilometres into the stage to Canazei, expecting, almost relishing, a violent reaction from the Italians packed along the sheer climb.

We weren't disappointed, although darkening skies spoilt my chances of recording the 'show' on film. But it was there for all to see - Visentini against

Roche, Roche against Visentini, Roche against Italy - if not record for posterity. A lot of what went on was incomprehensible to me, but it was most definitely intimidating to be surrounded by so many tempers running so high. One after another, the spectators gave vent to their feelings, gesticulating angrily as the group passed by or throwing missiles made from *La Gazzetta dello Sport* into the fray.

Many spectators, intent on

impressing their feelings on Roche at close quarters, ran a few metres alongside the group, dodging perilously between other spectators and Roche's 'minders', who numbered just two - Robert Millar and Eddy Schepers. It was on these two that Roche depended for protection; the rebellious Millar was a member of another team altogether, taking the opportunity to thumb his nose at the Italians (and maybe secure Roche's support in his quest for the mountains prize). Visentini, alarmed by the way his fans were reacting, did his level best to behave like a team leader, playing to the gallery, surging ahead at regular intervals to the delight of the spectators - and the millions watch-

ing on Italian television. Luckily, only a few projectiles found their mark, and at the 2001-metre summit the show came to an abrupt end; the *tifosi* were finally left behind as the Giro d'Italia - and its bandit-leader - plunged away from the Dolomites and onto faster, less dangerous terrain.

Unfortunately for us photographers - though not for the sport - such ugly scenes are rarely seen in cycling. Incredibly, since those dramatic few days in 1987, the Italian public has gradually taken Roche back to their hearts, reasoning that even if he hadn't been right to usurp Visentini,

Carrera team! - and Visentini has long since been forgotten.

Such explosive incidents are, however, rare. The Giro can be a very tame proposition, following as it does hard on the heels of the temperamental Vuelta. Whereas Spanish cycling is a growth industry, winning popular support

A human wall of emotion awaits to greet the 1987 Giro on the Passo Marmolada... and greet especially the race's new leader...

he had at least proved he was the better cyclist and by far the braver competitor. Riding with class in the mountain stages, then winning the decisive time-trial on the final day, Roche had finally shown the Carrera team and the *tifosi* just who was boss. Visentini, meanwhile, went from sore loser to non-finisher, abandoning the Giro in the last week. After the fuss died down, and in fact until his retirement in 1993, Roche was actually feted by the fickle *tifosi* whenever he rode in Italy - ironically, back with the same

nationwide, the Giro's image is locked in the past. The majority of spectators along the route clearly belong to a bygone age in cycling: they watch Bugno, Chiappucci, Chioccioli go past, but they see Gino Bartali and Fausto Coppi ... These days, the Giro is a gentle interlude before we embark upon the hectic pace of the Tour de France in a few weeks' time. Its closer proximity to the Tour usually ensures that the Giro has classier competitors than the Vuelta; climbers and sprinters are honing their respective skills as the Tour approaches. Yet sometimes even this isn't enough to get the passionate *tifosi* to rise to the occasion in anything like the manner of their fellow-Latins in Spain.

What the Italians have that the Vuelta doesn't is an impressive array of ex-world champions whose legendary feats prove that the Giro has made an indelible mark in the republic's sporting history. Most of these former *campionissimi* participate in the Giro today - whether as honoured guests, like three-times winner Gino Bartali, or in a working role, as 'technical adviser' Francesco Moser. Much is made of their historic exploits, a factor that highlights - and maybe explains - the slightly apathetic attitude of the present-day public towards its champions, an attitude reinforced by the way in which the elderly Italian cycling press presents the sport. When Franco Chioccioli blasted his way through the 1991 Giro, winning mountain stages as well as a time-trial close to the finish, the papers made at least as much of the fact that he was a mirror-image of Fausto Coppi as of 'Coppino's' masterly domination of the Giro.

These days, only Claudio Chiappucci and Gianni Bugno have the power to rouse the *tifosi*, and only the hard-core supporters travel to the mountain passes to cheer on their men. Chiappucci was a member of the Carrera team in the 1987 Giro and was the only Italian on the team to voice public support for Roche. Despite this, and his known dislike of Visentini, Chiappucci was obliged to toe the team line and help only Visentini - a role he interpreted, in the rebellious style for which he is renowned, by dropping off the pace as soon as the Marmolada climb began!. When Chiappucci wanted to win the Giro in 1993, it was Roche's turn to support Chiappucci, a role the Irishman relished during his final year as a racer, and which also made sure no one has forgotten the famous events of 1987.

All the same, with such a glorious history as a cycling nation, a few weeks on the Giro can be a very satisfying stroll

This hurriedly created graffiti summed up Italy's love-affair with Franco Chioccioli - the re-incarnation of Fausto Coppi - as seen on the side of someone's house at Broni, in 1991.

The Giro has its own ways of celebrating the last road stage each year. In 1992, the peloton saluted themselves - and *maglia rosa* Miguel Indurain - as they made their pedestrian way to Vigerano.

down memory lane. Along the route, and in any part of the country, memories of the past linger on in old photos on the bar-room walls. Nearly every mature Italian male has either raced a bicycle or known someone who has, and most casual conversations reveal a wealth of knowledge about cycling and the Giro - and, in fact, Italy's two classics as well. It's unusual for a Giro d'Italia to pass through the north of the country without connecting at some point with the routes of Milan-San Remo or Giro di Lombardia. Italy's dominant position in cycling is in evidence all the way, whether in the grand old days of Coppi and Bartali, or today's would-be *campionissimi* - Bugno and Chiappucci.

The route of the Giro varies every year, though there is always an obligatory, blisteringly hot trek south towards the heel of Italy and regular visits to Sicily before the race turns to the cooler, wetter north for the closing stages. Italy's mountain passes in the Alps and Dolomites provide the best racing terrain in the country, but it is also a fact that Italy's wealth is concentrated in the north. So it is before the citizens of Trentino, Alto Adige and Aosta that the Giro finale is

Former Giro winner Francesco Moser, chats with Miguel Indurain in 1993. A great time trialist himself, Moser's advise to Indurain was well received.

played out most years, enticing hundreds of thousands of spectators to the roadsides in their Lancias and Mercedes, their chic outfits a stark contrast to the workwear of the peasants of the south.

Along the route, whatever part of the country it passes through, streets, shop windows and bars are festooned with Giro regalia - this support for the Giro being inspired by the promoting newspaper's clever exploitation of its rose-coloured paper. The organisers of the Tour de France decided in 1919 to create the yellow jersey, to mach the colour of the paper on which l'Auto (renamed l'Equipe) was first printed,

and in 1931 the Giro d'Italia struck on the idea of distinguishing the race leader with a pink jersey exactly matching the pastel of *La Gazzetta dello Sport*. As a consequence, the *maglia rosa* became the symbol of Italian cycling, its popularity at an all-time high in the Coppi/Bartali years of the late-1940s. It became fashionable for villages and towns to decorate their streets in pink whenever the race passed through, with rusty old bicycles suddenly re-painted - in bright pink - and prominently displayed in the windows of all kinds of shops, or left at strategic street corners to catch the eye of the passing cyclists.

Gino Bartali still makes it to the podium in the Giro - forty eight years after he collected the last of his five victories! He's also a scene stealer, which is probably why neither Roberto Conti or Miguel Indurain seem very impressed with their 'guest' this time...

Nostalgia is in evidence all the way in the Giro, and not only amongst the cyclists. This ancient Fiat awaits to follow the Colombian cyclist, Luis Espinosa at the start of the big time trial of 1993, between Pinerolo and Sestrière. It's not known if the car ever made it to the mountain-top!.

In 1988, realising the publicity value of the *maglia rosa,* La Gazzetta dello Sport began a nationwide competition to decide 'the best-dressed window display of the Giro d'Italia'. Now, it's not just old bicycles that receive the treatment; just about anything goes - from Fiat 500s resprayed pink to dogs dressed up in pink lavatory paper!. Competition is high between villages and then between shops and stores to get the prestigious award. And if a village is so small that it doesn't have a shop window to decorate, it can always join in the fun as Rossana, in Piedmont, did in 1993. It's not an unusual sight to see riders' names painted on the road in Italy, but the residents of Rossana decided to paint the names of each of the 154 cyclists that started that day's stage from Varazze!. In reverse order of general classification, starting with last-man Mariuzzo, the painted names stretched for almost half a mile, or the length of Rossana's main street, before ending with the words: 'GRAZIE MIGUEL INDURAIN'.

Whereas the Tour de France is in a class of its own in terms of scale and popularity, it's hard to judge the Giro without making comparisons to the Spanish tour just completed. Sometimes barely a week separates Spanish *meta* from Italian *partenza,* and with Spanish impressions so fresh the mind slides inevitably into comparisons - of organisation, quality of racing, even food (pizza versus paella) and - most of all - the landscape, although it's impossible to say which is the more spectacular. Addicted as I am to the big tours, I'd never been able to

present myself at the start of any Giro until 1994, having usually arrived as the race made its way north, with twelve or fourteen days still to go. Of course, that two weeks would have contained the very best of the Giro, with at least two time-trials, a selection of sprint finishes, a chance to sample the fine wines of Tuscany, Umbria and Piedmont - and, most of all, breathtaking passages of the Dolomites and Alps.

But doing a full Giro for the first time opened my eyes to

Rossana, and its street of names, in 1993.

The Giro often crosses into neighbouring countries, such as here in 1990. Bugno, the race-leader shares the podium with stage-winner Allan Peiper in Klagenfurt, Austria.

the subtle pleasures of the race that had always gone unnoticed in my haste to make the most of a half-Giro. Now, rather than expecting an action-packed jamboree - and be quite often disappointed - I allowed myself to be carried along by the gentile ambience, enjoying the racing when it was there to be enjoyed, but happily switching off on the quieter days to take in the unforeseen delights of the Giro in Abruzzi, Campania and Lazio, and in particular the magnificent Palazzo dello Reale, alongside which a stage of the Giro ended in Caserta.

To any race-follower, the Dolomites sum up the Giro. Spectacular rocky spires tower above the valleys of Gardena, Ampezzo and Fassa, building up to the jewel in the crown: the Passo di Gardena, a sumptuous ascent offering the most spectacular scenery in Europe, almost completely unspoilt by tourism or ski resorts. The Giro returns again and again to this area, and one particular route has become something of a climbers' classic, with two

ascents of the mighty Passo Pordoi, separated by the monster climb of the Passo Marmolada - all in the same day!

This stage first appeared in the Giro in 1990, and was an outright success the following year, when the second climb of the Pordoi witnessed Chioccioli's masterful solo break, cheered to victory by an estimated half-a-million fans drawn

to the mountain by the 'Coppi-cat' publicity showered upon Chioccioli. In an almost identical stage two years later an equally impressive crowd turned out, though this time they were disappointed: Chiappucci trailed Indurain over the second summit, forfeiting the *Cima Coppi* prize traditionally awarded on the highest mountain in the race. Now that would

The Mortirolo Pass contains this quaint chapel on its northern side, but of more relevance is the fact that it is recognised as the hardest ascent in any of the great tours, with sections of the 12-kilometre climb as steep as 18%. The four cyclists in this picture had little time to digest this fact - for three of them: Massimiliano Lelli, Leonardo Sierra, and Claudio Chiappucci were about to watch *maglia rosa* Chioccioli ride away into the distant blue yonder.

never have happened in il *campionissimo's* day ...

If the Dolomites is unsurpassed for spectacular scenery, the Passo dello Stelvio in the Ortles Alps carries the emotional baggage of the Giro's heroic past, evoking historic images of courageous cyclists battling through gruelling conditions. The most heroic feats of the Giro - lone cyclists battling through walls of snow four metres high - seem to have taken place on the Stelvio. Coppi was one such hero in 1953, and his conquest of the 2758-metre mountain inspired the creation in 1963 of the *Cima Coppi* prize as the world of cycling mourned his sad death from malaria.

The Stelvio is also Italy's highest mountain pass, and very unpredictable in springtime, so the race route always contains a contingency plan should the

The race for the *Cima Coppi* is always competitive. Franco Chioccioli won the award in 1991, breaking away on the Passo Marmolada to arrive on the Pordoi summit as both stage and *Cima* winner. In 1994 it was Franco Vona (below) who got this most prestigious prize on the summit of the Stelvio Pass.

pass be closed. Despite the fact that the Stelvio had been on the route four times since my first visit to the Giro in 1986, it was only in 1994 that I finally discovered its spectacle - bad weather having previously forced the race to make a diversion away from the mountain, and usually when it needed the excitement of the Stelvio to enliven proceedings. It last saw action in the Giro in 1980.

In 1991, informed that the race was once again going to bypass the mountain because of avalanche risk, I took a break at a mountain restaurant along the revised route. As we sipped our *cappuccini* under a blazing hot sun that was nipping in and out of the scattered clouds, I could see the pass quite distinctly through a long telephoto lens and gave expression to my feelings about the decision. 'Nothing wrong with the conditions', I said to Ismael. 'We've been short-changed again ...' Barely had my words made sense to my Basque driver than a massive avalanche filled the view-finder, silencing my scepticism

The mighty Passo Pordoi in all its glory, in the 1991 Giro, as the leaders cross the summit for the first time. It's hard not to feel on top of the world as you follow the best cyclists in the world over the 2,223-metre summit, oblivious to the mechanical ugliness of the Giro's logistical equipment; when the Stelvio is unusable, this is the high point of any particular Giro.

once and for all. Just supposing that 170 of the best cyclists in the world had been on the mountain ...

But 1994 was the year I finally experienced this famous peak on a stage from Merano to Aprica that was preceded by days of hype and speculation in sports' newspapers all over mainland Europe. But with the climb coming barely one-third of the way through the race, it did little to change the leading positions, and Franco Vona, as ever the opportunnist, raced away to take the coveted *Cima Coppi* in front of a substantial crowd, the majority of whom would have had to have camped out on the freezing mountain all night to see this segment of modern Giro history being made. Had this been a stage-finish, there would have been ten times the number of people up there, all of them enjoying a grandstand view of the show, for the Stelvio's last ten-kilometres are stepped through a series of *lacets* with a bend coming approximately every 500-metres!

Miguel Indurain had tried to turn this day into a legendary story for himself, having started from Merano in third place overall, three-and-a-half minutes behind the Russian whizz-kid, Evgeni Berzin. Following a

thirty-five kilometre descent from the Stelvio, the favourites arrived at the foot of the Passo del Mortirolo with Vona still a few minutes ahead, and with an assortment of chasers between the Italian and Indurain's group. Berzin attacked immediately, pre-empting the expected surge from Indurain, and for a few kilometres rode about 100-metres ahead of his challenger. But Indurain never let go, and soon pulled the Russian back, by this time passing what had been the chase behind Vona, who himself was passed by Berzin and Indurain. When Indurain accelerated again, only two cyclists were still ahead, and Berzin had cracked, at last, and thus began what seemed to be a legendary escape a la Coppi...

After the Mortirolo descent, Indurain quickly picked up the remaining escapers on the valley road and the two gratefully accepted Indurain's superior pace as a way to move into the top places overall. The gap to Berzin continued to grow, quickly to a minute, then ever-so slowly to just over two minutes - a clear sign that Berzin was letting go. Indurain led the trio through Aprica to start the last twenty kilometres, with the 1994 Giro seemingly in the palm of his hands, though we were soon to realise the effects that the Stelvio had had on him, in conjunction with the stiff headwind through which Indurain had been pacing his 'guests' up the valley.

An intricate descent after Aprica led to a tiny right-turn

onto the shaded Valico di Santa Cristina, and then the full impact of Indurain's effort hit home - he fell to pieces! Normally this tall, elegant, athlete rides in one fully fluid motion, his long arms and legs working so systematically to compliment the capacious lungs for which Indurain is reverred. But at this moment, his arms and legs - still not yet conditioned for an effort such as this - let the lungs down badly, and Indurain was unable to maintain the pace that at one point had seemed to be capable of taking four minutes from Berzin. Instead, it was Pantani who profitted, realising his luck as he flew away beneath the trees to eventually win into Aprica and take second-place overall.

Behind, Indurain was a sorry sight, left also by Rodriguez now, and soon to be passed by none other than Claudio Chiappucci, who'd been left for dead on the Mortirolo. Luckily, Berzin himself was in trouble on the Santa Cristina, and therefore unable to completely

close the gap to Indurain who swept numbly into Aprica with a measly gain of just thirty-odd seconds over the *maglia rosa.* The day we'd waited fourteen years for was over - the Stelvio had been climbed once again. The day we'd waited years for, to see Indurain attack in the mountains, was over too - and while it lasted that had been sensational. I comforted myself with the knowledge that today had been the 'queen' stage of the Giro - and what a stage..!

Out of the mountains, the Giro's racing style can be thoroughly pedestrian at times,

hour after endless hour at less-than-tourist speed. To the hapless captive spectator, *'gruppo compatto'* seems an expression invented solely for the Giro. Sometimes the pace is so dull that the tour organisers have been known to play classical music over the race-radio in an effort to stifle our yawns. But when there's no music, all we hear is '... *gruppo compatto ...'* It's a phrase you're never likely to hear in the Vuelta, with its infamous turn of speed, nor in the Tour de France, where competition is so fierce the only way to sort

Come on Thierry, it's not that bad... Well established within the 'laughing group' that climbed Mont Monviso in 1992, Thierry Marie plays the clown once again, as befits this endangered species of the professional cyclist that simply cannot climb mountains as fast as Miguel Indurain. Is his fooling an act, or simply a way to divert the agony for a few moments?.

out the men from the boys is to ride flat-out! But then what the Giro lacks in excitement, it more than makes up for in the flamboyance of its riders: neither the Vuelta nor the Tour have had the pairing of Mario Cipollini and Alessio di Basco to brighten up a dull day ...

I first came across di Basco in 1987, arriving in Italy for the finish of the stage to the Adriatic resort of Jesolo. I just had time to grab my credentials and take my place on the finish line before the race came in. It was only when I focused on the intact seething peloton bearing down on me at 40 miles an hour that it dawned on me I shouldn't really be kneeling down in the road; like my colleagues, I should be poised in a watchful genuflection, ready to leap out of the way before the 'animals' crossed the line. But by the time I'd registered this it was too late, and a blur of metal, coloured fabric and sweat came at me, glancing off my leg as I leapt for the cover of the television tribune. The one that came closest probably never knew anything about it, and thankfully has never learnt my name. Yet since that day I have kept a

Alessio Di Basco (above) and Mario Cipollini (right) are two of the most colourful characters of the European peloton. Fast, charismatic, and - when need dictates - downright sadistic, they are the playboy sprinters of the Giro, playing to a public bored with the *'gruppo compatto'* syndrome - expectant of a tumultuous finale to any flat stage. Vigevano, 1992 (below): Di Basco finishes second again to Cipollini.

wary eye on Alessio di Basco...

In the modern Giro, sprinters like Cipollini and di Basco keep the race alive on the monotonous flat stages when a mass sprint is clearly the *piatta di giorno.* Not content to wait for the last hour's accelerations, and the showdown in sight of the finish line, they start their two-man show in the first few kilometres, laughing and joking at the back of the peloton, throwing food and water at every *gregario* unfortunate enough to move into range, and generally amusing the entire caravan. When the race heads into the mountains these flamboyant characters are suddenly silent and reserved, aware of the torture lying ahead for physiques entirely unsuited to climbing. Yet come the day when the flatlands are once again on the agenda - and in the Giro the majority of days are like this - di Basco and his younger 'twin' are back in their element.

Their crude displays of aggression are not a device for our amusement, however. They are a signal to the timider souls in the peloton that the day

Chiappucci and Indurain are as inseparable in the Giro, as they have been in the Tour de France. Here the pair climb a mountain high above Lago Maggiore, on the way to Verbania in 1992.

belongs to the sprinters, and they had better stay out of the way later. Sure enough, in the last few kilometres, and in the presence of the all-important live TV, we see another side to their characters. Fighting for position, elbows and fists flailing - and sometimes feet too in di Basco's case - they terrorise their rivals with a mixture of physical and mental intimidation as the finish line approaches. Their undoubted friendship forgotten, Cipollini and di Basco go to war on each other, and on any other cyclists foolish enough to enter the most dangerous of cycling lists, the mass sprint. In the final metres our two Tuscans are usually one and two - nearly always in Cipollini's favour - and afterwards there are usually official protests about their dubious

tactics. Myself, I prefer to observe the macho men of cycling and their battles through an ultra-long telephoto lens ...

Blood-curdling sprints and magnificent scenery aside, the Giro can be undeniably dull, especially if it's followed on from a totally absorbing Vuelta. One reason for this is that, in spite of the fact that every other cycling nation has thrown out the 'one team, one leader' philosophy, Italian racing is stuck in this outmoded class structure. It is still possible to be just a *gregario* in an Italian team, and as such riders are not encouraged to do more than support their leader. Many foreign teams look upon the lethargic Giro as a welcome respite before the rigours of the Tour de France; after all, it's

up to the Italians to make the racing in their own national tour ... But the Italian riders are often reluctant to punish themselves, and this opens up the Giro to ruthless exploitation by a passing maverick such as Miguel Indurain, who in 1992 won the Giro simply by destroying the opposition in the time trials: the rest of the time he cruised along '... *piano, piano* ...' with the peloton ... a style his successor Evgeni Berzin adopted in 1994.

Life on the Giro is a life of extremes; days so exciting you never want them to end, and other days I don't want to remember for fear of diminishing my enthusiasm for the sport. I love the Giro, of that there is no doubt, but I don't know why: when I try to analyse it too many conflicting memories come to mind. Dreary miles of *'gruppo compatto'* punctuated by fresher memories: the first time I set eyes on the Giro in 1986 in the cobbled square of Piacenza, when Francesco Moser roared home to a tumultuous welcome in a time-trial from Cremona; my narrow escape from death in Jesolo at the hands of di Basco in 1987; seeing the Gardena Pass for the first time in 1986; the superb Chioccioli in 1991; Indurain's domination of the 1992 edition. The most abiding memory, though, is of Stephen Roche making faces to the hostile crowd in Canazei in 1987, just a few hours after alienating all of Italy with his humiliation of Visentini on the Marmolada. I owe to Stephen my introduction to what racing in the Giro should be like. Thank you, Stephen ...

Stephen Roche stops for a chat on his way back to the peloton in 1987 - a few days before he took on Visentini, and won. His ever-smiling face will be a lasting memory for me as long as I continue to follow the big peloton.

When Claudio Chiappucci joined an attack at the start of a stage to Sondrio in 1992, Miguel Indurain just had to follow, enlivening what might otherwise have been a dull stage from Aprica. Here the pair race to the limits, playing out their escape to the full on this short stage, and with original attacker, Alessio Di Basco! tucked well in behind. Another shot with fill-in flash, this picture gains additional strength because of the looming backdrop - giving a clue as to where the action was taking place.

CAMERA
Bronica ETRs
LENS
75 mm Zenza
FILM
50 ASA
SHUTTER
1/500 flash
APERTURE
f 5.6

Macho men Alessio Di Basco and Mario Cipollini bare their chests at each other during a quiet stage of the 1992 Giro, amusing themselves - and me - before the more serious stuff began. When I'd begun to take this photo, it had only been Cipollini talking to a team-mate. Then Di Basco wheeled by, demanding that he too was worthy of some attention, and the show commenced!. It is moments like this that photographers treasure the most - for they don't occur very often!.

CAMERA	
Bronica ETRs	
LENS	
75 mm	
FILM	
50 ASA	
SHUTTER	
1/500 flash	
APERTURE	
f 5.6	

Words can do little to adequately describe scenery like this. This is the awesome Passo di Gardena, at the heart of the Dolomites, and I'm in the process of using about four complete rolls of film such is the magnificence of this particular part of the stage. Although the peloton was tightly grouped as it began the climb, a factor that usually disappoints any photographer wanting to pass the group for a good vantage point, on this beautiful day the cyclists seemed aware of our needs, obligingly letting us slip past time after time, all the way to the top. Thanks guys!.

CAMERA
Nikon F4
LENS
16 mm Fisheye
FILM
50 ASA
SHUTTER
1/250
APERTURE
f 8

Sprinters are by nature a
tough breed of men, and
they needed to be in the
1994 Giro when there was
a crash during three of the
six 'sprinters' stages.
Roberto Pagnin fell at
Bibione within sight of the
line, but was already
rinsing his wounds out with
his water bottle by the time
medical staff - and the
fittest photographers - had
run the 100-metres to
reach him.

CAMERA
Bronica ETRs
LENS
75 mm
FILM
50 ASA
SHUTTER
1/500 flash
APERTURE
f 5.6

Gianni Bugno was a
revelation in the 1990 Giro,
winning all three individual
time trials, including this
one at Cuneo. His style will
never win him an award for
elegance, but on his good
days, Bugno is one of the
fastest cyclists around.

CAMERA
Nikon F4
LENS
300 mm
FILM
200 ASA
SHUTTER
1/500
APERTURE
f 2.8

Laurent Fignon crowned his successful 1989 Giro with this superb piece of sprinting into La Spezia, just a few days before the race ended in Florence. Behind him in the sprint are all his rivals for the Giro - Maurizio Fondriest, Flavio Giupponi, Phil Anderson and Andy Hamspten, with Erik Breukink and Marino Lejarreta obscured. You only have to look closely at Fignon's eyes to appreciate the Frenchman's hard-fought success after nearly five years of relative failure. Yet nobody then could have predicted the battle he was to have with Greg LeMond in the forthcoming Tour de France...

CAMERA
Nikon F4
LENS
180 mm Nikkor
FILM
100 ASA
SHUTTER
1/500
APERTURE
f 5.6

97

CAMERA
Bronica ETRs
LENS
75 mm Zenza
FILM
100 ASA
SHUTTER
1/500 flash
APERTURE
f 8

'Eh, *gelati*'... Italians are mad about their ice-creams, so why should cyclists in the Giro be any different..?. Franco Vona (left) tucks into this monster *cornetto* before a stage-start from Verbania in 1992, while Switzerland's Daniel Gisiger apparently popped into a shop during a quiet stage to Vittorio Veneto in 1988 and bought himself this *piccolo cornetto*. He shows no intention of sharing it with his friend, does he..?.

CAMERA
Nikon F3
LENS
135 mm Nikkor
FILM
100 ASA
SHUTTER
1/500
APERTURE
f 4

CAMERA
Bronica ETRs
LENS
75 mm Zenza
FILM
50 ASA
SHUTTER
1/500 flash
APERTURE
f 4

The Giro certainly exudes its country's tastes for flambouyance, and how often it is always the sprinters who seem to be the showmen - on and off the bike. Guido Bontempi seems on the point of arrest in this picture (above), but more likely the uniformed gentleman is about to escort one of Italy's most popular cyclists into a group shot with his colleagues of the Carabinieri, at Corvara in 1993. Stefano Allochio gatecrashed the pre-stage 'live' television show in Dozza in 1993, and turned himself into a cameraman in order to share some of Bruno Leali's attention as race-leader.
Roll camera..!.

CAMERA
Bronica ETRs
LENS
75 mm Zenza
FILM
50 ASA
SHUTTER
1/250 flash
APERTURE
f 4

Miguel Indurain had trouble from another of Argentin's clan in 1994 - Evgeni Berzin - and was forced to go on the attack like never before in order to win the Giro for a third time. I made sure to be right there when the Spaniard put his big attack in on the Passo del Mortirolo, guiding my driver to within a few feet of Indurain's gasping face. At this point, I thought the Giro was all over, so strongly did Indurain pull away from his young rival. Yet in a thrilling finale to an exceedingly thrilling day, Indurain himself cracked, allowing Berzin to regain almost all his deficit by the finish.

CAMERA
Canon EOS1
LENS
80-200 mm zoom
FILM
50 ASA
SHUTTER
1/250 flash
APERTURE
f 4

It's not mere co-incidence that the Tour has become a truly worldwide phenomenon since the participation of Greg LeMond in the early-1980's. The American's presence attracted unprecedented media interest from around the world, and events like his defeat of Hinault in 1986, his spectacular victory over Fignon in 1989; and LeMond's own fall from glory in 1991 and 1992 - all this has fed a drama-hungry public for almost a decade.

ten days before the first mountains, a period that seems to pass so slowly given the sense of expectation ten days beyond when the Tour will really be fought out. Yet those opening days represent for many what the Tour de France is really all about in terms of combativity and razz-a-matazz, with a fresh plot each day fuelled by the ambitions of nearly 200 cyclists to win just one stage.

And what a jolt! One can't expect to be startled by the so-staged prologue, but the first road stage sends shock-waves through the system with so much intensity around us. Even the well-chaotic entourage of the Vuelta pales into a non-event in the aftermath of a Tour

lity are there for certain in the Vuelta and Giro, but the vintage Tour has been carefully allowed to ferment into what it is today and what its cousins may well never be - a player on the world's stage. And the immense differences are there before one's even fired-off the first picture-frame....

To settle into the race requires arriving no less than 48-

hours before the traditional prologue time-trial in order to regain the working mode so carelessly flung aside after the Giro. But actually one never really settles into the Tour at all, so imposing is the race on a day-to-day schedule that never quite seems adequate or felxible enough to comfortably digest the pressures placed on it. A 'normal' Tour starts at least

The ONCE team's one great ambition is to win the Tour de France team time trial...they came second in 1993.

An inevitable crash: a race-official's motorbike lies in the road on the last stage of the 1993 Tour, an innocent victim of race-congestion.

de France peloton seemingly trying to rip itself apart. Instead of the habitual presence of half-a-dozen photographers' bikes in the Vuelta and Giro comes a prestigious clique of sixteen - fighting for places behind the race with six radio bikes and five television, while lamely attempting to comply with the Tour's overbearing regulations as to what can - and can't - be done in pursuit of our trade. It is in these first days that one really notices the enormous differences between the Tour and any other race, with a pace so frenetic that disaster seems to be perpetually just a pedal-stroke away.

Each and every kilometre is fought over by the riders as would be a classic in Belgium or France, with equal passion being applied by the Tour's so-awesome entourage that numbers seem as determined as each cyclist to assert supremacy over one another. Even to a race-hardened follower, the pressures of working in the wake of the peloton in the first day or two are overbearing, only letting up when the traditional team-time-trial enforces some order to the whole affair after two or three days. Before that point, the dog-eat-dog world behind the peloton is an all-consuming occupation, with photographers forever at the mercy of feverish *directeur-sportifs* barging their way through our indian-file in order to pamper to their riders' every needs, or debating some point or another with an over-strained official.

But the biggest impression comes when one tries passing the peloton to get to the finish in the first few days, a peloton hell-bent on putting each of its members in with a chance of sprinting to the line first - and to hell with anyone else!. When one is forced to spend the last 65-kilometres of a stage in the wake of a screaming pack of pedalling animals, to have tried edging nervously along the half-metre-wide strip of tarmac separating animals from a sudden drop into a ditch, to have got halfway along the pack travelling at 70-kilometres-an-hour only to be spat backwards by a chorus of abuse and physical threat from the animals, to become nauseous through the smell of 200 sets of brake-blocks stopping their charges from a mass pile-up...it is only then, finally, that the intensity of the Tour really sets in.

Each of the first days can be like this in an average Tour, making for a tense atmosphere every step of the way. In 1993, in a Tour that had each and everyone of the world's best sprinters on their marks, I missed two consecutive stage-finishes in the opening week, simply unable to pass in the last hour so intense was the racing. Even the team-time-trial did little to ease things that year, with rival sprinters' teams jealous that Mario Cipollini, the fastest sprinter of all that year, had got himself the *maillot jaune* thanks to the efforts of his Belgian-Italian MG-GB team. Only when Indurain cooled everybody's ambitions with his expected demolition job at the Lac de Madine time-trial five days later did the Tour finally settle down, and that on the eve of its entry into the Alps.

Come the mountains and suddenly everything that happened in the opening week is completely forgotten, submerged in the speculation and excitement that the outcome of the Tour is about to be decided. Truly, a new race is about to start, a race very different from that one just ended, a race where characters almost unoticed in the first week or so suddenly spring to the fore, launched centre-stage by their ability and determination to defy gravity. Whereas on the flat stages one could only judge the peloton as a whole, now, in the high-country, the protective envelope of the peleton falls away to reveal individuals alone against the mountains. Some emerge triumphant; lesser athletes meet their destiny in the form of the *voiture balai*, or the evil time-keeper; the least fortunate end up in a hospital bed.

It's here that the overpowering media which has probed, cajoled and speculated its way through the opening week in search of a story or picture when there never really was one, finally settles into another, more refined mode of working - one where stories of triumph and tragedy come delivered almost on a silver-platter, or at least a press-room computer or television. And it's here that the connoisseur-photographer finally realises his fantasy of working the mountain stages again, free from the constraints and frustrations of the flat stages, where now his or her flirtation with nature is allowed to blossom - usually in the form of a 20-kilometre climb to a mighty 8,000-foot-high snowy Alp. The Tour de France was made for the high mountains of the Alps and Pyrenees - the only natural stage where the might, emotion and energy of the race finally meets its maker...

Tradition has it that a vintage Tour is only found when the Pyrenean stages precede those of the Alps, a romantic

belief based on the fact that the Pyrenees were first climbed a year before the Alps, in 1910, and that the peloton loses some of its equilibrium should it hit the south-western mountain range last. Until the mid-1980's it would have been hard to argue with the fact that the best Tours did seem to come when the Pyrenees were tackled first. Yet recent Tours have utilised a clockwise direction more and more, throwing up memorable battles in both mountain-ranges - and thus defying any of that earlier belief. Nevertheless, given the Tour's vintage history, it can seem odd when the strategic pshycological barrier of the Alpe d'Huez is diluted by its placement in the routing as one of the first climbs, instead, as is usual, as one of the last...

Of course the mountains contain the most romantic history of the Tour, so insurmountable and life-threatening did it seem when the Tour first set wheel on

These two German cyclists were in trouble during an early, very fast, stage of the 1992 Tour. Uwe Ampler changed bikes, and was almost paced back to the peloton by his teamate Bernd Gröne when the speed got too much. In desperation, Gröne resorted to a crude handsling to get Ampler across the widening gap. But for Gröne there was to be no return. The youngster can only watch helplessly as the Tour pulls inexorably away, leaving him hopelessly behind, and eventually out of time.

Claudio Chiappucci rode into everyone's hearts with his performance on the Col du Tourmalet in 1990 - his own heart surely inspired by the legend of this mountain in years gone by.

Though less extensive, the intricacy of the Pyrenees offers perhaps greater prospects of drama - especially if the Tour is entering its final week. The classical Pyrenean route is to go over the Col d'Aubisque, Col du Telegraphe, Col de Peyrousourde and Col d'Aspin, imitating that historic stage in 1910 that became known as 'the ring of death', thanks to some creative reporting by the Tour's journalist-founder, Henri Desgrange.

In modern times, the Tour has found an equally classic route by throwing in a ski-station finish such as Luz-Ardiden, Pla d'Adet, Guzet-Neige or Superbagnères - depending whether the stage has run east or west - and created another day's racing by using a circle of climbs like the Col de Burdincurutcheta, the Col Bagargui and the Col de la Marie-Blanc in a stage that will inevitably start or finish in Pau - one of the Tour's most regularly visited cities.

In the Alps, the Tour can choose to enter from the north - using one of the sheer ascents that make up the Massif de la Chartreuse; from the west, rea-

the fearsome slopes of the Col du Tourmalet in 1910. Having survived the Tourmalet, and in a day that had also included the passes of Aspin, Peyresourde and Aubisque, the Tour quickly spread its wings into the Alps, 'conquering' the mighty Col du Galibier one year later, even though the roads they used then were little more than cart-tracks. Along with the infamous Puy de Dome, the Tourmalet and Galibier now form the backbone of what connoisseurs would consider the classical Tour route, running preferably anti-clockwise around the country to reach the Pyrenees after about ten days by which time there will already have been a team and individual time trial of considerable length to give some order to the classification, as well as fair distribution of flat stages for the sprinters.

Two climbing days in the Pyrenees is the considered minimum to set the Tour up nicely for the grander Alps, with a three or four days' interlude in the south or centre of the country to separate France's two mountain ranges. Whereas the Alps offers a plethora of potential five-mountain stages - enough to race over for ten days if the Tour so wished - the more idyllic Pyrenees has perhaps as few as two suitable stages, needing occasionally to dip into Spain or Andorra to expand its potential.

A fog-shrouded Luz-Ardiden welcomed the Tour in 1985, and saw a great battle between the Colombians Parra and Herrera. Herrera came second that day, and is seen here nearing the finish, resplendent in his polka-dot jersey.

Robert Millar was one cyclist who just couldn't wait for the mountains to begin. Here he climbs the Col de la Marie-Blanc in 1986, co-incidentally pacing LeMond towards the summit in an effort that was to help LeMond win the stage at Superbagnères and take over the race-lead from Bernard Hinault.

ching the Vercors plateau by way of the stunning Gorges de la Bourne; or from the south and south-west via such delights as the Col d'Allos or Col de Vars. Whichever combination the Tour selects to gain access to the heart of the Alps, once there it utilises the highest peaks to an almost sadistic extent, throwing legendary peaks like the Col du Glandon, Col du Telegraphe, Col du Galibier and Alpe d'Huez into one single stage - or taking an equally mind-boggling route over lusher, greener climbs like the Col du Joux-Plane, the Col de Saisies or Colombière, before striking eastwards onto something like the Col d'Iseran as the Tour did when it visited Italy in 1992, throwing in the Col du Mont Cenis along the way for good measure before the ten-kilometre finale to Sestriere.

1993's epic stage was the crossing, in one single day, of the Col d'Izoard, the Col de Vars, and the awesomely exposed Col de Restefond before making its debut at the ski-station of Isola 2000 in the Alpes-Maritime. And this the day after having subjected the riders to the hellishly steep north face of the Galibier! Though the Tour continues to find new, or relatively unused climbs - Luz-Ardiden was 'discovered' as late as 1985 - it proudly sticks to the famous climbs that have shaped the very character of the race, relinquishing none of its sporting legend in the face of a galloping commercialism. But in recent years, the Tour's geography has had to be re-defined in light of an enforced shortening of the race's length by the sport's governing body, a factor that has led to the Tour having at least one major transfer-leg in order to maximize the influence of both Alps and Pyrenees, and still get around the country.

This fore-shortening has also depleted the possibility of using the notorious climb of the Puy de Dome for, depending on whether the Tour has spent more than a week reaching the Alps or Pyrenees, a choice routing is to go between each mountain range over the Puy de Dome, or alternatively prolonging the agony and suspense by utilising the vicious single-track ascent en-route to Paris. The freak giant of the Auvergne became a legendary Tour landmark after the battle between Raymond Poulidor and Jacques Anquetil in 1964, where the two French stars banged and barged their way to the summit in a spectacular battle for the Yellow Jersey, though Fausto Coppi had initiated the Puy's *legende* by winning the first Tour ascent in 1952.

1978 was no less spectacular, with soon-to-be-crowned hero Hinault losing disastrously to both Michel Pollentier of Belgium and arch-rival Joop Zoetemelk in the arduous time-

125

The Puy de Dome saw a monumental battle in 1978, between Dutchman Joop Zoetemelk (top) and French hero Bernard Hinault - with Zoetemelk coming out on top in the gruelling time-trial.

a passage over the 1,909-metre summit, with a long swoop into Carpentras for the finish.

So much speculation and expectation is placed on the mountain stages that once they're past there seems to be little that can remotely excite either peloton or press. It's while waiting for the next mountain passage - whether it be Pyrenean or Alpine - that for the first time even experienced Tour-followers lose their way, hoping forlornly that the transitory stages will throw up some unexpected drama or incident to enliven a period still reverberating from the first spell in the mountains. It's in this period too, that the cyclists show the first signs of exhaustion as the effects of mountain racing begins to permeate their frail physiques. The quiet days between mountains are the most hazardous for a Tour cyclist - the unusually long, hot stages playing games with their mental constitution as they come off the surge of adrenalin that helped carry them through the pain of climbing.

Depending on the damage inflicted by the opening mountain stages, the second phase can be either brilliantly spectacular, or a total anti-climax as much depends on the character of the *maillot jaune*, who will dictate the way the final obstacles are raced. For three years on the trot, from 1991 to 1993, Miguel Indurain arrived at the second mountain phase already safely established as an unbeatable Tour leader, and wanted nothing more than to keep everything quietly in order before his final display of time trialling a few days later. His countryman Pedro Delgado was similarly dominant when he exited the Alps in 1988, but

trial up from Clermont-Ferrand. Now, as if deliberately seeking to ration its spectacle, the Puy is visited only once every five years at the most, its extraordinary once-volcanic summit known by so few of today's current racers.

Relatively unexploited, but by far a more legendary ascent, is the Mont Ventoux, first used by the Tour as late as 1951. Known locally as the 'balding giant of Provence', the Mont Ventoux has been used less than a dozen times in the seventy years its road has been open, achieving the utmost notoriety in Tour fable by virtually killing Britain's Tom Simpson, who collapsed and died on the exposed mountain in 1967. The Ventoux is one of a select number of mountains in France where memorial plaques have been fixed to commemorate some of the Tour's heroes - Simpson's is placed exactly at the point where he conceded his life. But the Ventoux's location, close to the tourist-saturated Rhone valley, makes it a nightmare of a stage-finish for the modern Tour with its 3,500-strong travelling army. Its role in the 1994 Tour was restricted to chose to use the last climbing stages - a Puy de Dome ascent following two spectacular stages in the Pyrenees - as a playground for his devastating form, powering away on all three summit finishes in the most aggressive display of climbing seen in years.

By far the most thrilling climax came in 1989, when the Alps delivered what seemed to be the final verdict on a Tour dominated by just two men - Laurent Fignon and Greg LeMond. Having started a memorable battle in the Pyrenees, LeMond and Fignon took to the Alps in a devil-may-care fashion, with LeMond regaining the Yellow Jersey at the Orcieres-Merlette mountain time trial, losing it the very next day to Fignon at L' Alpe d'Huez, losing further ground on the short stage from Bourg d'Oisans to Villard-de-Lans where Fignon struck a brilliant stage-win - before scoring a brilliant sprint win at Aix-Les-Bains, after LeMond, Fignon and the next three on general classification had broken clear of the peloton in the last moun-

Scenes of Mont Ventoux: (top) spectators line the final few hundred metres in the 1987 time trial, won in convincing style by France's Jean-Francois Bernard (bottom picture). Before the race began, former director Jacques Goddet laid a wreath at Tom Simpson's monument.

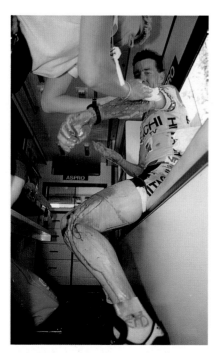

The heat takes its toll in the last week: Jos Haex (above) crashed on roads covered in melted-tar and had to abandon the race in 1989. A young Laurent Fignon (below right), finds a new use for Perrier water as he cools off after a stage in 1984.

ders all day a wiser, more entertaining choice, is to sometimes await the stragglers halfway through one stage, sampling a fascinating process of elimination, calculation and - for some - salvation, as the sprinters seek the most comfortable, secure way of staying in the race one more day. It's not just for their sprinting prowess that Green Jersey winners are hailed as second-only in importance to the actual winner of the Tour...

And then suddenly it's all over. A dash to Paris follows a time trial that's probably been of interest to only half-a-dozen cyclists, and their still-clinging entourage of jaded journalists. There follows a major culture shock as one comes to terms with life in the French capital

Greg LeMond won into Aix-les-Bains in 1989, to set up a great finale in Paris a few days later against Laurent Fignon.

tains of the race. So great had been their battles, that the 1989 Tour was already oustandingly memorable before the now-famous time trial in Paris where LeMond struck a final, devastating blow.

For many, the last few days of a Tour de France are a burdensome experience, only salvaged by a finale like that in 1989, or by the chance to re-kindle a somewhat forgotten interest in the Tour's severely-reduced posse of sprinters. Throughout the mountain-stages it is these men, the swash-buckling heroes of the first week, who will have run their own private battles with fate in an attempt to survive through to contest the grand-finale in Paris. As memorable as the climbing may be in a typical mountain-stage, rather than stay perpetually with the lea-

after three weeks of rural bliss, and which prompts a hurried, panicked exit as soon as possible after the sprinters have done their job. While for some, a celebratory supper in a chic left-bank *bistro* is the preferred 'epilogue', elongating an evening dedicated to one's own survival of another Tour de France, while paying dutiful respect to the cycling heroes that induced our tour in the first place. Was it a vintage one? It will be Christmas before an accurate assesment can even be considered... The final word must rest with a great american friend of mine, Louis Viggio, whose sinful words during the 1993 Tour - "this race sucks!" - have condemned him to a life of moutain-biking in the USA, from which there will be no return ... *Vive le Tour*!

Djadmoline Abdujaparov is a three-times winner of the Green Jersey points competition and one of the few sprinters who actually enjoys tackling the mountains. He's seen here in 1991, climbing the Col du Soudet in the Pyrenees.

CAMERA
Canon EOS 1
LENS
80-200 mm
FILM
50 ASA
SHUTTER
1/250 flash
APERTURE
f 4

Britain's Chris Boardman shocked the cycling world with his 55-kilometres-per-hour performance in the 1994 Prologue time trial in Lille. The GAN rider, in his first Tour de France, beat Miguel Indurain and Tony Rominger to become the first Briton to wear the leader's symbolic jersey since the late-Tom Simpson in 1962.

Sean Yates continued the English flavour of the 1994 Tour, racing into the Yellow Jersey just one day after 'Le Tour' left England to return to France. Here, the Sussex hero cuts a fine figure on the road to Futuroscope, thoroughly enjoying this special day in his life. There couldn't have been a more popular wearer of the Yellow Jersey, so much has Yates earned his colleagues' respects in an eleven-year career.

CAMERA
Bronica ETRs
LENS
75 mm
FILM
50 ASA
SHUTTER
1/500 flash
APERTURE
f 5.6

There couldn't be two more different winners of the Tour than Laurent Fignon and Miguel Indurain - and their contrasting emotions in these pictures seem to illustrate that. Fignon is seen on the attack (below) trying to put the 1989 Tour out of LeMond's grasp for good... while on the left we see our luckless hero winning a stage at La Plagne in 1987.

Indurain is photographed on the Col du Galibier in 1992, calmly defending his maillot jaune against all-comers, and against the spectacular backdrop of the Meije glacier.

CAMERA
Bronica ETRs
LENS
75 mm
FILM
50 ASA
SHUTTER
1/500 flash
APERTURE
f 5.6

CAMERA
Bronica ETR

LENS
75 mm

FILM
100 asa

SHUTTER
1/250 flash

APERTURE
f 4

The Fall Of An Idol: Greg LeMond's Tour victories of 1986, 1989 and 1990 must have seemed worlds away for him when he blew up spectacularly on the stage to Val Louron in 1991. And his face mirrors his emotions, as well of those around him as he arrives at the finish (left). Yes, Greg LeMond really is a normal human being... Things were no better in 1992, worse in fact, and LeMond is in trouble on the climb of the Col du Galibier on the stage to Alpe d'Huez. For this great champion, there's nowhere to hide as LeMond contemplates quitting - something the drama-hungry media knows only too well...

CAMERA
Bronica

LENS
75 mm

FILM
50 asa

SHUTTER
1/500 flash

APERTURE
f 5.6

CAMERA
Bronica ETRs
LENS
75 mm Zenza
FILM
50 asa
SHUTTER
1/500 flash
APERTURE
f 5.6

Andy Hampsten always dreamed of winning a Tour stage at Alpe d'Huez - and his dream came true in 1992, capping a day when, finally, it all went right for the American. His path to glory (left) is guided by the masses of people squashed into the last three-kilometres - and in particular by a Swiss cyclist carrying the stars and stripes. This picture more than any other, shows the difficulties of photographing the finale at Alpe d'Huez, where there is simply no room for error by anyone of the motorbikes clustered behind Hampsten. Somehow we made it past in time for the finish, where Hampsten arrived in a cauldron of emotion, undoubtably the happiest man alive that day!

CAMERA
Nikon
LENS
180 mm
FILM
100 asa
SHUTTER
1/500
APERTURE
f 4

As expected, Miguel Indurain dominated the 1994 Tour, exploding the race with a devastating time trial at Bergerac, then continuing his assault in the mountains of the Pyrenees. Even though his supposed challenger Tony Rominger had already faltered, the explosion of power and determination Indurain displayed during the Pyrenees made it very obvious that the outcome would have been little different had Rominger been at his best. Indurain's pace to the summit of Luz-Ardiden was the highlight of my 1994 Tour, not least as it provided me with this memorable shot of the champion in full cry

CAMERA
Bronica ETRs
LENS
75 mm
FILM
50 asa
SHUTTER
1/500 flash
APERTURE
f 5.6

The two days which 'Le Tour' spent on English soil in 1994 turned out to be one of the highlights of that year's event, with massive crowds lining the lanes and highways of southern England. Like everyone else, I was overwhelmed by this passionate welcome to the race, and spent the two days in frenzied action driving from location to location seeking out the photograph that would best sum up England's hosting of the great race. Ditchling Beacon was the favoured vantage point for tens of thousands of fans, and I managed to steal a place amongst them to take this shot as the race approached its finish in Brighton.

CAMERA
Bronica ETRs
LENS
75 mm
FILM
100 asa
SHUTTER
1/250
APERTURE
f 4

And it's not only the hierarchy who get to wet their whistles either. There is stiff competition amongst we snappers to be the one alongside the top man's car when the cork pops - then to look decidedly thirsty - then to catch Leblanc's sympathetic eye. A few years ago, Jorg Müller, the experienced Swiss cyclist, happened to be passing back to the peloton just as this discreet charade was going on. 'Ah, champagne!', he yelped excitedly ... These days, on the stroke of noon, it's curious how often you see Müller casually slipping off the back of the group, apparently in need of a mechanic or a pee-stop! Fortunately for Leblanc, this is a secret Müller has kept from his colleagues.

Of course there is another, more serious, side to Jean-Marie Leblanc's character. Step out of line in one of his races, and you'll have to watch your step for quite a while to come. In all the events organised and controlled by the Sociètè du Tour de France, Leblanc runs the race - fairly, but vigilantly, overseeing the conduct of us motorbike photographers. Leblanc is familiar with each of the èlite sixteen, having worked with us previously, both as journalist and race director, and prior to that had himself been a professional cyclist. For the most part, he trusts us to make our own decisions, like when and where it's safe to shoot, or at which point to make our precarious way across a particularly turbulent peloton ...

The single-mindedness of cyclists with a bunch sprint in sight - indeed their competitive instinct in general - is far more evident in the Tour than the other big tours. In fact, if you added together the killer ins-

"These Alps aren't so hard, after all.." Javier Murguialday and Jacky Durand sneak a tow from a television motorbike during a quiet spell in the racing, in 1992.

tincts of the Vuelta and Giro you would still have nothing like the competitiveness that pervades every piece of action in the Tour. But it is precisely that sense of occasion - that 'buzz' of anticipation - that puts us all on our mettle.

On a Tour stage in 1993, knowing that the last 35 kilometres would be where the racing really took place, I'd opted for waiting behind the intact peloton as it raced flat out across the Orne landscape towards Evreux. I was alone in this conviction, all of my colleagues having read the race correctly and moved in front; still, I stuck to my guns until we reached saw the '20 kilometres to go' sign - at which point I caved in and motioned to my driver to start moving through. But the

30-team peloton had smelt a bunch sprint, and no sooner had we moved into the fray, than the pace went from fast to crazy, then to absolute boiling point - more than 65 kilometres an hour. Leblanc having granted my request to go in front, Rafa flexed his muscles and began squeezing the BMW through, muttering Basque imprecations at the cyclists he knew, and coolly ignoring the warnings from other cyclists to go back.

Five times we got halfway up the group that was riding verge-to-verge at suicide pace. The fourth time we almost made it, only to be blocked by the live TV bike that just couldn't find space to pull over and let us by. The fifth time I cracked, frightened to death of

177

causing a crash. The last time was the worst - my nerve went completely - but what shocked me most was being subjected to physical violence by some of the cyclists. Cyclists who that very morning had been fooling around in our slipstream, laughing and joking with us, now glared at me wild-eyed, thumping me as we drove along-

More wine Monsieur..?
A spanish cyclist risks a bad ride by drinking Muscadet, a few minutes before a stage in the 1988 Tour.

Two of the most popular characters, Jean Marie Leblanc and Stephen Roche discuss the day's news during a stage in 1992.

side; others literally spat their protest at our efforts to get by, obviously angry that we should be choosing that moment to try. Resigned to failure, we fell back. I caught Leblanc's eye. 'Are you still here?', he seemed to be asking, a wry grin just detectable at the corners of his mouth.

This mutual trust makes for a fine atmosphere during the quieter moments of a race, and a good relationship- usually - with the cyclists, officials and my colleagues is another element of the pleasure I get from photographing the big tours. In a one-day classic this kind of relationship is impossible - they're over too quickly for the necessary ambience to develop. Over the three weeks of one of the big tours, though, a kind of intimacy has a chance to develop. On a given day you can find yourself in conversation with a 'star' cyclist that you happen across while traversing the peloton; or if he's not interested in conversation you can be the butt of his joke. In the

last days of a big tour, when you're trying to coax a reaction from what by then is a very tired athlete, the rapport you've established previously can prove invaluable.

It's uncanny how often, in moments of high tension, a top rider will stare straight at the face he knows best - ignoring the half-dozen other lenses focusing on his mask of pain as he climbs one big mountain after another. And if you're really fortunate, it might be enough, just once in a while, to persuade Indurain to remove his big black glasses. I've only managed this once - on the run-in to Paris at the end of the 1991 Tour - and in any case, a cluster of my colleagues cashed in on the precious moment as well.

Photographing a stage race differs greatly from a one-day classic. By contrast to a classic's six or seven hours of non-stop action, most of which you spend struggling to keep pace with the cut-and-thrust of the racing, uneasily aware that you're only going to get one chance at a shot, working on a three-week-long event is an altogether more satisfying experience. For one thing the weather is getting better, while the action evolves more gradually - allowing time to savour certain moments, and to plan the next move. Then the landscape we pass through is constantly changing, opening up limitless possibilities for photographers. And most of the time you have the reassuring knowledge that this isn't the only picture you'll be able to take of a particular cyclist, not unless he's just chosen that moment to fall on his head at 30 miles per hour - in which case it may well be the only picture you need

Tony Rominger, Miguel Indurain and Zenon Jaskula head for the summit of Pla d'Adet in 1993.

stayed together, it's a dodgy business getting too close to the group - the pace can increase abruptly if the group chooses, enveloping an incautious motorbike. In any case, the action in the closing stages is only of interest to the newspaper photographers that have daily deadlines to fulfill; unless there's a crash, nothing in the last hour will change to the overall situation, so there's no need for magazine photographers to get involved. The finish picture is our principal concern on the flat stages: calculating whether it'll be a bunch sprint, a late breakaway, or a freak lone victory. Each possibility affects our choice of equipment at the end.

For safety reasons, these days photographers are allowed no closer than ten metres from the line; a far cry from a few years ago when that dis-

Miguel Indurain kisses the bride, a few minutes before starting the stage to Oropa in the 1993 Giro. Nobody knows if the *maglia rosa's* spirit gave the happy couple a great start - but it was to be a nearly disasterous day for Indurain, who saw half his lead wiped out on the final climb.

tance was down to our own choosing. Things are fairly straightforward in the Vuelta and Giro, save for the odd *tifoso* that sneaks his way into our secure area. In the Tour it's a very different story because so many hundreds of people congregate around the finish area, to say nothing of up to 100 photographers wanting a finish shot, especially when a bunch sprint is the most likely finale. The Tour organisation has formulated a somewhat èlitist policy for this contingency, with the twenty 'most important' cameramen placed ten on each side of the road starting ten metres from the line, and forming a V-shaped funnel through which the cyclists are expected to squeeze after they've crossed the line.

The motorised traffic ahead of the race is also expected to shoot through this funnel. This comprises the lead car with Albert Bouvet aboard, as well as one motorbike and a car that follows the race home. If it's scary for us - watching through a telephoto lens as a

The strong men of the Vuelta bear down on the line in Avila, in 1992. A few seconds after this shot was taken, Tony Rominger rode into a wayward television cameraman, severely bruising his left shoulder - and sending the expensive machine crashing to the ground.

The mob gathers for another sprint finish in the 1991 Tour de France.

shiny red car doing 120 kilometres per hour comes hurtling at us - it's a great deal worse for the next twenty photographers in the pecking order, ten metres behind our lines, and with an almost clear view of the finish. Having passed through our V-shaped wedge without incident, this is exactly the point the lead car is making for... After all that, even in days of super-fast sprinting, the reflex action of firing the shutter as the cyclists streak home is something of an anti-climax.

Elite or not, every single photographer reserves his best efforts for the mountains, where he can budget for the use of twice as many films as a day on the flat. And it is here, having watched the newspaper and agency photographers blitz the flat stages for more than a week, that the magazine photographer comes into his own. The drama of the mountain stages doesn't alter the daily deadlines of a newspaper man: every day he must send a black and white shot of the finish, as well as the day's most important action. But for the colour 'artist', the mountains are an incomparable canvas - matching the splendour of snow-capped peaks with the cruellest test of a rider's physical and mental constitution.

The photographer's day will pass in a blur of nervous energy, as he prepares and then tries to carry out his carefully prepared plan. He'll wake too early, due to the adrenalin rushing through his sleeping form, and will almost certainly have had trouble getting to sleep in the first place. If he's a perfectionist he will have scrupulously cleaned all his equipment the evening before, a ritual that only takes place in the mountains. Finally, he'll present himself at the start at least thirty minutes earlier than usual, having dragged his indignant driver out of bed to show he means business. But then any good driver will have experienced similar upsets to his metabolism in anticipation of the day ahead.

Of course, our photographer won't be alone in his nervous state - everyone else on the race is altered by the prospect of seven hours in the mountains - not least the cyclists, for whom the prospect may not be quite so exciting. Once on the move, the air of nervousness is heightened as we try to settle into our planned routine, all the while distracted by the sight of cyclists steeling themselves for their day. If the first mountain is within sight of the start there won't be a single rider dropping off the back, not for a pee or anything, so anxious are they to get to grips with the climb. Only at the front will there be any action, and this is where most of the photographers are to be found, a few hundred metres in front, constantly looking back to see which team is controlling the race - and therefore who we can expect to focus on when the hammer goes down.

Until it goes down, at what will be a fairly obvious point - the first really hard climb - we must bide our time, hovering just ahead of the race. Perhaps we will risk a scenic picture from the side of the road, but we've waited so long for the mountains we are not about to let ourselves get trapped behind the race, missing the action up front. But when the field begins to fragment, perhaps through one climber's acceleration, or another's failure to respond, we spring into action, releasing a wave of adrenalin and concentration that can use up a roll of film in seconds. When this doesn't happen - when the field continues to stay together over more than one big climb - we know it's going to be an unproductive day, with everything decided by the last climb. But if we see a few heroes dancing away from the front, it is our signal that the big guns are all set to go off.

It would be hard to devise a more perfect working day in the mountains than stage 10 of the 1993 Tour de France. The action broke early during the 204-kilometre bash from Villard-de-Lans to Serre Chevalier, and resulted in everyone taking the racing on until the crux of the Col du Galibier where the race exploded. This early in the mountains it was an unexpected treat, and the race officials were so delighted at the prospect of a great day's racing that we had no restriction on how we worked, either from the bike - creeping alongside for a few seconds, or

hovering a few metres in front - or by jumping off on every other hairpin bend of the gruelling 19-kilometre pass. I'd never had so much licence to work creatively.

It was the same story the next day to Isola 2000: another great day's racing unfolded before our lenses. But by contrast, one week later in the Pyrenees, what should have been the toughest stage of all turned out to be the biggest anti-climax of the whole race. A total of five huge ascents in the

course of 230 kilometres from Andorra to Pla d'Adet should have been guaranteed to bring the race to a boil one last time. Instead, the entire peloton rode like snails for the first 160 kilometres, even to the extent of retaining its few surviving sprinters over the 2000-metre summit of Puerto de la Bonaigua. Only in the last hour, over the minuscule Col du Portillon, did

The Col d'Izoard is one of the few mountains to have seen action in both the Giro d'Italia and Tour de France. Fittingly, there is a memorial on its southern flank to two of the sport's most heroic characters - Italy's Fausto Coppi, and France's Louison Bobet. The memorial is placed along the section of the Izoard called the Casse Desert, and it was a modern Italian hero, Marco Pantani, who was first past the memorial in the 1994 Giro.

the stage come alive, and our spirits perked up as the 7-kilometre ramp to Pla d'Adet drew near.

But our normally obliging race officials, clearly frustrated that the peloton had wrecked such a potentially great day's racing (and maybe a little irascible from too much champagne - it had taken more than seven hours to reach the Col du Portillon) became obstructive, and our work got increasingly difficult as the final ascent began. As always, Bouvet's car was guarding the front of the race, but as he sensed our determination to retrieve a bad day by capturing the last mountain finale this normally even-tempered official started to shriek at us over the race radio. With Bouvet's driver doing his best to prevent us getting behind his car - and therefore out of his control - I

and most of my colleagues determined to outwit him, risking a whole race's goodwill in our desperation to make something out of the day. Some of us slipped back when his attention was with another photographer, others simply stopped at the roadside between clumps of spectators. I went for this method, urging Rafa over to the verge, but Bouvet's driver spotted us and drove into the side of the bike, almost tipping us over. But my plan had worked, and we moved onto the narrow road in front of Rominger and Indurain as they stormed up the climb, and for the next 25 seconds I hogged centre-stage, shooting off a whole roll of film in my excitement. I ate and drank well that evening, pleased to have got the best pictures of the stage, and perhaps of the race as well. Though tomorrow's stage

Puuush... Italians stick together whenever they are racing on foreign soil. A cyclist from a rival team contributes his strength to pushing Gianni Bugno up the Col de la Bonaigua in the 1993 Tour de France.

was to take us over the north face of the Col du Tourmalet and the Col d'Aubisque, we were not expecting anything exciting - the race was all but run, and in Indurain's favour. Nevertheless, exciting was how it turned out, and not only in terms of the racing.

We'd set off for the start at Tarbes well ahead of schedule, expecting a photographers' protest. Bouvet had issued a *communiquè* the previous afternoon condemning our behaviour at Pla d'Adet, but our view was that he'd lost his temper unreasonably, and that given the number of people at the roadside his driver had driven in a dangerous manner.

There was no strike - something the more militant French photographers favoured - as Bouvet withdrew his *communiqué*, apologising for his aggression in the heat of the moment. But I knew nothing of this until later; Rafa and I were standing on the road to Tarbes contemplating a sick motorbike. 'Problems?', I enquired, observing a jumble of metal fall away from the rear wheel. 'El freno', the Basque replied, indicating the severity of the problem by pretending to slash his throat. We'd lost the use of the back brake, a reflection on the severity of the descents of the past week. Removing the remains of our braking mechanism for good, Rafa set off to intercept the race on its approach to the Tourmalet, with me on the back contemplating the prospect of descending such a sinuous pass with no back brake.

Going uphill was no problem, and we had a good morning's photography as Rominger went on the attack for the last time, opening a gap on Indurain of a kilometre or more near the summit, which let us get right up close to the gasping Spaniard. But the summit marked the end of our fun, for we simply couldn't follow Indurain down the mountain - something I would have relished, for I knew Indurain would make the most of his swoop after Rominger. Waiting until the main rush had gone by, Rafa pronounced it safe to go down, and we began one of the most nerve-racking descents I ever hope to make, expecting any moment to hear that our front brake had gone as well ...

So life as a photographer on the big tours is not without incident, sometimes within the race or, as just described, almost out of the race; there's not a single day in either the Vuelta, Giro or Tour that doesn't contain at least one memorable moment. That it takes place in the company of such a wonderful array of humanity, people cast in much the same mould as myself - adventurers - makes it all the more worthwhile. But of course I couldn't do it without so many others.

Most especially, it is the drivers who have enabled me to fulfill my passion, and the list is long indeed - I hope it isn't a reflection on the way I treat you all! To Philippe Bourguet, my first-ever Tour de France *motard* in 1987, to Jan Wouters and Gèrard Montigny who each did a Tour, to Patrice Diallo who shared the Vuelta and Giro with me in 1990, to Ismael Borges who for the last four years has chauffeured me on both Vuelta and Giro; and of course to Rafa Landa, known affectionately as 'the beast of Bilbao' - thanks for the memories.

Travelling companions, Ismael Borges (left), Rafa Landa, and photographer Frèderic Mons, pose at the roadside during a Tour de France stage.

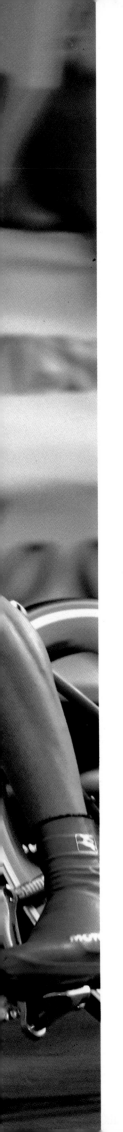

As this is a book aimed predominantly at the cycling enthusiast, I've not wanted to interrupt the text with descriptives about the technique and equipment used to capture the 200-odd photographs in The Great Tours. Those of you who are interested will already have studied those technical details supplied - and for the benefit of people wanting to know more, I'll try and expand on my theory here. I work using two camera formats - 35 mm and medium-format (6 x 4.5cm). Since the start of 1994, I've been using the Canon EOS1 system for the 35mm format, having changed from Nikon after more than fifteen years. This change was for practical reasons, allowing me to photograph cycle-racing with just four lenses - 15mm fisheye, 20-35mm zoom, 80-200mm zoom, and 300mm f2.8 - whereas as with Nikon I needed to carry up to nine lenses to cover the same focal parameters.

For the medium-format photography, I have been using the Bronica ETRs with a 75mm lens since 1986, and before that a similar camera from Mamiya - the 1000RS, with a 70mm lens. Both these cameras are perfectly suited to the use of fill-in flash, as their shutters sychronise at 1/500th of a second. Though there have been great advances in the optical quality of some 35mm format lenses, there is still a significant advantage when using fill-in-flash at 1/500th of a second over most 35mm cameras that operate at a maximum of 1/250th of a second and may exaggerate any blur caused by the slower speed. But it is the size of the film that attracts the most with medium-format, offering studio-quality images of one of the most colourful outdoor sports in the world.

Cycle racing is a constantly moving sport and takes place over the most varied and demanding terrain. As such, the photographer has to be an absolute master of his or her equipment, in order to capture this beautiful subject, and still be able to deal with the rigours of moving with the race. The 35mm system is of course more vestatile than medium-format, and allows the photographer to record scenes from a variety of angles and perspectives - using the four lenses to their maximum - and to focus on the action as soon as it happens. Together, the Canon and Bronica systems give me maximum flexibility and scope in a sport that was never designed for the confines of a stadium ...

My film stock these days is made up entirely of Fujichrome, both in 35mm and medium-format size. Through its RDP, Velvia, and now Provia emulsions, Fujichrome has virtually taken over the market in professional sports photography. The density of its colours and versatility in exposure, has made our work so much more enjoyable and presentable. In an average Tour de France I will use up about 250 rolls of film, which is almost double the amount I'd need for either the Giro or Vuelta, a fact that reflects on the increase in combativity in the Tour - and that combativity is between the photographers!.

VUELTA A ESPAÑA

1935 Gustave Deloor (Belgium)
1936 Gustave Deloor (Belgium)

1941 Julián Berrendero (Spain)
1942 Julián Berrendero (Spain)
1945 Delio Rodríguez (Spain)
1946 Dalmacio Langarica (Spain)
1947 Edwar Van Dijck (Belgium)
1948 Bernardo Ruiz (Spain)

1950 Emilio Rodríguez (Spain)
1955 Jean Dotto (France)
1956 Angelo Conterno (Spain)
1957 Jesús Loroño (Spain)
1958 Jean Stablinski (France)
1959 Antonio Suárez (Spain)

1960 Franz De Mulder (Belgium)
1961 Antonio Soler (Spain)
1962 Rudi Altig (Germany)
1963 Jacques Anquetil (France)
1964 Raymond Poulidor (France)
1965 Rolf Wolfshohl (Germany)
1966 Francisco Gabicagogeaskoa (Spain)
1967 Jan Janssen (Netherlands)
1968 Felice Gimondi (Italy)
1969 Roger Pingeon (France)

1970 Luis Ocaña (Spain)
1971 Ferdinand Bracke (Belgium)
1972 José Manuel Fuente (Spain)
1973 Eddy Merckx (Belgium)
1974 José Manuel Fuente (Spain)
1975 Agustín Tamames (Spain)
1976 José Pesarrodona (Spain)
1977 Freddy Maertens (Belgium)
1978 Bernard Hinault (France)
1979 Joop Zoetemelk (Netherlands)

1980 Faustino Rupérez (Spain)
1981 Giovanni Battaglin (Italy)
1982 Marino Lejarreta (Spain)
1983 Bernard Hinault (France)
1984 Eric Caritoux (France)
1985 Pedro Delgado (Spain)
1986 Alvaro Pino (Spain)
1987 Luis Herrera (Colombia)
1988 Sean Kelly (Ireland)
1989 Pedro Delgado (Spain)

1990 Marco Giovannetti (Italy)
1991 Melchor Mauri (Spain)
1992 Tony Rominger (Switzerland)
1993 Tony Rominger (Switzerland)
1994 Tony Rominger (Switzerland)